Bob Laurent has realized that the real Jesus can't be contained solely within the four walls of Sunday-church Christianity. As a vital part of the Good News Circle, he spreads the ever-new Word across the land. He talks—and knows—of a faith dependent on discovery, not just dogma . . . and of a new knowledge of Christ that brings jubilant liberation and a life filled with love.

What is Bob Laurent saying?

"Christianity is not a religion, it's a relationship."

"God never told the world to go to the church. He told the church to go to the world."

"I've discovered that Jesus is not the namby-pamby milktoast deity that lets me sit in church and sing 'Just As I Am' and remain just as I was."

Growing numbers of Christians have listened and found new meaning, new life. In these pages you will learn why—and how.

What a Way to Go

Bob Laurent

David C. Cook Publishing Co.
850 NORTH GROVE AVENUE • ELGIN, IL 60120
In Canada: David C. Cook Publishing (Canada) Ltd., Weston, Ontario M9L 1T4

WHAT A WAY TO GO

Copyright © 1973 David C. Cook Publishing Co.

All rights reserved. Except for brief excerpts for
review purposes, no part of this book may be reproduced
or used in any form or by any means—electronic or
mechanical, including photocopying, recording, or
informational storage and retrieval systems—without
written permission from the publisher.

David C. Cook Publishing Co., Elgin, IL 60120

Printed in the United States of America
Library of Congress Catalog Number: 73-78714
ISBN: 0-912692-20-0

To the memory of Dave Michael, a Godly man whose whole life was a call to happiness. Dave flew me in his own plane to a secluded spot in the Adirondacks to write this book. A few weeks later, on Thanksgiving Day, he suffered a fatal crash in his Cessna 320. But don't feel sorry for Dave. He's still flying high. He just doesn't need a plane anymore.

Signs of Life

Introduction

ONCE UPON A TIME, in a far-away land, a lovely young virgin was in for the surprise of her life. Out of nowhere an angel appeared to her and shouted, "Congratulations, favored lady! The Lord is with you."

She was greatly disturbed and confused by what he said, but the angel told her, "Don't be afraid, for God has decided to wonderfully bless you. Very soon now you will become pregnant and have a baby boy, and you are to name him 'Jesus.' "

The angel went on to tell Mary things about this Son of hers that made her heart pound even harder:

"He shall be very great and shall be called the Son of God. And the Lord God shall give Him the throne of his ancestor David. He shall reign over Israel forever; His kingdom shall never end!"

The lowly servant girl sat there amazed. This was a dream to end all dreams. Without even wishing on a star, Mary had been given a blessing almost too good to be true. After all, things like this happen only in fairy tales, and the Brothers Grimm weren't even in the neighborhood of Nazareth that day.

Mary looked at the angel and said, "I am the Lord's servant, and I am willing to do whatever He wants. May everything you said come true."

Then the angel disappeared and Mary watched her dream become reality.

Isn't it tragic that so many people, from that first day to the present, have treated this living story of Mary's boy and God's son as a foolish fable? After you read WHAT A

WAY TO GO, I hope you will no longer be able to afford this luxury.

This book is not about fantasy because it is about the Man who said, "I am the truth." Its business is not to escape reality but to face it and slay the giants called Deceit, Bigotry, and Apathy. Giants may exist in fairy tales, but they also can be found lurking behind musty old pews and even masquerading as stalwart "defenders of the faith."

I read once that the human mind is like a parachute: in order to function, it must be open. I ask you to get into these pages with not only an open mind, but an open heart. You might get your toes stepped on, but that's all right. Jesus is the Great Physician: He can heal your feet!

The highway that winds through our lives has a fork in it. One road leads to confusion and emptiness, and millions are fooled into following it to their death. But the other road leads to an exciting adventure in living, and its travelers can often be heard exclaiming, "What a way to go!"

Elgin, Illinois   BOB LAURENT

*"For there is no other way than the one
we showed you . . ."* (Galatians 1: 7 LB).

ONE DAY JESUS took Peter, James, and John to a mountaintop. Suddenly Jesus' face began to shine with glory, and His clothing became snow white, more radiant than Miracle White could bleach them.

There He stood, white as snow. Not the man from Glad, but the Man from God.

Surely this must have bolstered the three disciples' belief that Jesus was the Messiah. They could rest secure because they had seen that the man they were following was really the living God.

But secure they were not.

Peter, the strong-willed fisherman, and the sons of thunder, James and John, were acting as if they had just seen Night Gallery. They were scared to death.

POOR PETRIFIED PETER

Poor petrified Peter, when will you learn?
When will you see more than just a dash of
Robin Hood in your mysterious leader?

11

When will you see who He is?

You must be tired of His embarrassing you.
Do you remember when Jesus told you to take your
boat into deeper water and that if you'd let
down your nets you'd catch a lot of fish?

Your reply was, "Come on, Sir.

We worked these waters hard all night and
didn't catch a guppy.

Besides, who're the professional fishermen
here anyway?

But if You say so, we'll give it a
try."

So you dropped your net over the side and it
filled with fish so fast it began to tear.

I wish I could have seen your face when you
had to call your buddies to come to help.

Then everyone needed saving because both
boats were so heavy with fish that they
were on the verge of sinking.

When you realized what was happening,
you cried, "Oh Sir, please leave us.

I'm too much of a sinnner to have
around."

I'll bet Jesus smiled a little in those early
days as He watched your reactions to His power.

But that smile must have appeared
less

and

less
as your faith grew
smaller

and

smaller.

You saw lowly water become wonderful wine and

your mother-in-law healed of a high fever.

What would it take to make you believe?

Or do you remember when you and the disciples were
fighting heavy seas one morning?

Suddenly you looked up.

Jesus was coming, walking on the water.

Somebody screamed, "Great Caesar's ghost!"

But Jesus said, "Don't be afraid boys."

Do you remember saying, "Sir, if it is really You,
tell me to come over to You, walking on the water."

And Jesus said, "Come on in. The water's fine."

How excited you were when you slipped over
the side and began to tread the waves.

That's when everything went wrong.

You turned your eyes from Jesus and
sank

hook,

line,

and sinker.

Jesus could only say, "Oh man of little
faith, why did you doubt?"

Will it convince you when you see Jesus raise
Lazarus from the dead?

Will you finally come around when you witness
a blind man wash the mud from his eyes and for
the first time take in the Light of the World?

Or will you know Him as God when in the
middle of a terrible storm you look on
helplessly as He stands strong against the
raging tempest and thunders:

"Quiet down!"

And roars at the sea:

"Be still!"

But in those last few hours before the Cross, you

13

will prove that you never did know Him.

You will swear everlasting loyalty, but a
courtyard of people will hear you badmouth
your Lord when He needs you most.

And as your cursing reaches its peak, you
will "hear" Jesus saying,

"Peter, dear Peter.

Didn't you walk with Me for three
years, living the miracles and knowing the love?

Didn't you swear you would follow
Me anywhere, even to your death?

Didn't you promise you would
never deny Me?

Oh man of little faith,

Why

do

you

doubt?"

PUT YOURSELF IN PETER'S SANDALS

It wouldn't be hard for me to put Peter down for his lack
of faith and to declare that he wasn't the spiritual giant
he was made out to be.

But I can't get off that easily.

His sandals fit me too well and my memory is not so
short that I can't remember having reacted to Jesus for
years with my own "pygmy piety."

I was a very "religious" guy, traveling for a Christian
college and evangelizing the country with my guitar, my
wife, and two good friends. Then one day in a Southern
Ohio church camp, my dishonesty caught up with me. I
came back to my tent in the afternoon and was con-

fronted by three people who meant more to me than anyone else in the world. They had caught me in a lie—not
a big lie—just a little white one.

I couldn't rationalize enough about it to make the pain
go away. The shock of having to face the fact that I was
a liar was too much for me. Dressed in only my swim-
ming trunks, I ran out of the tent with tears in my eyes
and headed for the woods. I crashed through the branches
and underbrush until, exhausted, I came to a little creek.
I decided there to have it out with God once and for all.
I yelled at Him for a long time, telling Him that I wasn't
going to believe in Him anymore.

"I'm tired of being a fake! If this Christianity thing
doesn't work, I don't want any part of it! Who do you
think You are anyway? GOD?"

Then I plopped down in the water and shut up for a
while. The longer I sat there, the more I realized that I
had talked to Somebody, and the more ridiculous it
seemed not to believe in the existence of someone you
can talk to.

I still felt awfully guilty, but I sat there silently in the
rippling water.

THE "UN"-WAY

For years I had talked about Jesus' ultimatum to the
Christians at Laodicea. It was one of my favorite Bible
axes and I had loved to grind it in the churches: "You
are neither hot nor cold; I wish you were one or the
other. But since you are merely lukewarm, I will spit you
out of my mouth." Now I saw myself in the mouth of
God! And as I sat in the water I became very aware of
His presence. Goose bumps dotted my flesh. I never considered myself a mystic and had never conjured up a

15

spiritual rendezvous with the supernatural. But I did know that I was being loved and forgiven. I couldn't deny it. Jesus was there.

There was no way I was going to miss out on His kind of love. I had finally reached that first important road sign. It read ONE WAY and I knew then that it was the only way to the happiness that most men only dream about. If He wanted me, I was His. But I had a new vision of what it meant to live for Him. I knew I couldn't be wishy-washy with Him or pussyfoot around His challenge. Just like Peter, I had been around Jesus, but I didn't recognize Him for Who He was. Traveling down this road can be a frustrating experience. It's a miserable way to go. I call it the "un"-way. But finally I could say I know Whom I have believed!

To Out-Duke the "Duke"

The superficial days are behind me now and good riddance. I've discovered that Jesus is not the namby-pamby, milk toast deity that lets me sit in church and sing "Just as I Am," and remain just as I was.

He is not the visiting cosmetics lady who couldn't heal chapped lips let alone leprosy.

Jesus was a muscled carpenter who grew up pounding nails and building houses. He was the revolutionary young man who stepped onto the porch of the Temple and out-duked John Wayne as He sent the greedy moneychangers and their tables sprawling to the floor. He made a whip out of ropes and drove the cattle, sheep, and oxen out of His Father's house while the guards and the crowd stood dumbfounded, not daring to speak out against Him.

He never claimed to be a nice guy; He claimed to be God.

Those who heard Him firsthand concluded that
no man ever spoke like this Man.
I am the Vine; you are the branches.
I am the Bread of Life; he who comes to
Me shall not hunger.
And he who believes in Me shall never
thirst.
I have been given all authority in Heaven
and earth.
I am the Light of the World.
The world's sin is unbelief in Me.
Before Abraham was, I am.
I am the Way, the Truth, and the Life:
no one comes to the Father but by Me.
I am the door: if anyone enters by Me
he will be saved.
I am the Son of God.
I am the Resurrection and the
life: whoever lives and believes
in Me will never die.

These are not the words of Mahatma Gandhi, or
Gautama Buddha, or Joseph Smith. Only Jesus made
these claims and lived up to them. He never said He was
Baptist, Catholic, Presbyterian, Methodist, or Pedestrian.
He never said you could get to Him by going to semi-
nary or by studying your Sunday school lesson. He
doesn't love the Pope or the president of the Southern
Baptist Convention any more than He loves you or me.

Jesus Christ is not here to take sides;
He's here to take over.

I Can't Say It's Hurt Me

One beautiful spring afternoon, a friend and I were

pricing a new van for the Good News Circle. Our old 1963 "Green Latrine" was ready for the rapture.

We had prayed that we would get a good deal and were primed for anything to happen. As we were looking in the show window at a real knockout, a crafty salesman spied me. As he angled his way over, he checked me out, no doubt trying to figure how a tacky young whipper-snapper like me could afford an expensive vehicle like that. I was almost ready to take up an offering when he noticed I was wearing a button which read "Jesus Christ changed my life."

He raised his eyes to mine and said, "Christianity, huh?"

I started counting my chickens as I thought, "Hot dog! This guy is a Christian brother and he's going to sell us this van at cost!"

Then he continued, "I've been a Christian for 63 years. Can't say it's hurt me. Can't say it's helped me."

I was disappointed and furious. After that line I completely forgot about the van.

"Good grief, mister," I replied. "I've been with Jesus for only a couple of years, but I'm so excited about living for Him that my body can hardly stand it. You can sit around these cars for 63 years, but that's not going to make you an automobile. And you can sit in church for 63 years and that's not going to make you a Christian. You must not know who Jesus is or you wouldn't have said what you did."

THE MAN NOBODY KNOWS

This is exactly the problem: not knowing who He is. In the past several years the Good News Circle has visited hundreds of churches and spoken with thousands of people about Jesus. Most of them are unbelievably confused about His identity. To so many Jesus is a dim, shadowy figure Whom they may have heard about around a camp-fire, in a worship service, or in others' testimony.

That's fine for others, but what about you? Are you growing weary in your search for this Jesus, and beginning to doubt that there really is such a God? Your problem could be like mine. I used to miss out on Jesus until it hit me I was looking for the wrong person.

The Jesus I'd heard about wasn't anyone I would introduce to the guys on the track team, because He probably couldn't run the mile under ten minutes. He was nobody I could tell the guys on the football team about either, because His frail little frame would probably fracture if He was ever tackled. And I sure couldn't tell any of the girls I knew about Him, because they'd laugh when they found out He was more girlish than they were.

Was I ever wrong.

As David Hubbard writes in *The Man Who Made Us Human*:

> When you think of Jesus Christ, you should say, "What a man!" But we usually make Him too sissified when we think and talk about Him. Those hardened fishermen would never have followed Him if He had been a pansy. We see real masculinity in Jesus Christ. Yet here was a Man who was also gentle with women. A prostitute dumped herself at His feet. He had no need to recoil from her in mock self-righteousness, and He had no need to exploit her. You and I would have been tempted both ways, but Jesus Christ in His freedom could treat her as a person."

"EAR YE! EAR YE!"

Jesus was often heard to say, "He who has ears, let him hear." It meant a lot to Him that people understood what

19

He said. I guess He thought that if they could grasp what He said, they would know who He was. It's amazing that so many ears right around Him didn't seem to work.

Take Judas Iscariot.

He was as good a guy as the next, and was even treasurer of Jesus' evangelistic team. He was in on the Kingdom's work from the ground floor. He had seen the miracles and known the Lord personally. And yet, for 30 silver pieces he doublecrossed the only perfect man who ever lived, the only genuine good-guy in the history of the world.

Why did you do it, Judas?

"Because, Jesus, your public relations are awful.

You could have been great, but You blew it every time.

Do You remember those two days when You fed over 9,000 people with just a few loaves of bread and couple of blue gill?

We could have called a press conference and built You up and made headlines all over Palestine and Rome, proving Your social welfare program was better than the emperor's.

With me as Your campaign manager we would have easily taken every primary and elected You president.

"But no. After You fed them, You told everyone to go home, and You went up into the hills to pray. I can't understand You.

When You came to Jerusalem, it could have been sensational.

The crowd was in Your back pocket, ready to make You king.

If only You would have let us
carry You in on a throne or
a rented gold chariot.
"But not You.
No, You made us get You a donkey.
Jesus, You could have been a somebody but
You settled for being a nobody.
I can't forgive You for that.
"And the things You said.
You told us that if we're slapped on one
cheek to turn the other,
to forgive seventy-times-seven times,
that if someone takes our shirt, to
give him our coat as well.
"What nonsense.
You told us to love our *enemies* and to do
good to those who *hate* us.
That's insanity.
It's certainly not how wars are won—
or football games,
or family fights,
or elections.
"Jesus, don't You know they're going to string
You up for saying things like that?
You told us that the first shall be last
and the last shall be first.
But that's not true.
It's first come, first served.
It's not blessed are the meek for they shall
inherit the earth.
*It's blessed are the filthy rich for they
already own this earth.*
It's not blessed are the pure in heart for
they shall see God.

*It's blessed are the powerful for they
sway votes and control lives.*
It's not blessed are the peacemakers for they
shall be called the children of God.
*It's blessed are the crafty and greedy for
they shall know how to get ahead.*
It's not blessed are the persecuted for righteousness' sake for theirs is the Kingdom of
Heaven.
*It's blessed are the pious fakes and reli-
gious snobs who play word games with God and
live for themselves.*
"Jesus, don't You see?
We had to crucify You.
You
asked
too
much."
No, Judas, Jesus asked for the only thing He could
He asked for everything. It may seem like too much to
give but listen closer to what Jesus is saying:

"For if you give, you will get! Your gifts will return
to you in full and overflowing measure, pressed down,
shaken together to make room for more, and running
over. Whatever measure you use to give—large or
small—will be used to measure what is given back to
you" (Luke 6: 38 LB).

I heard it said once that "no man is a fool who gives
what he can't keep to gain what he can't lose." Who could
you trust with your life more than the living God? "You're
in good hands with Jesus Christ" and you won't be bored
with Him because He will invest your life in problems all
around you.

22

God is not a Santa in the sky who will allow you to serve both love and hate, war and peace. He is actively involved in this world for good and is aware of the ugly realities that stare at us from all sides.

Soon after the lottery system was used with the draft, I was driving along an expressway one morning when I was startled by a billboard which read, "Happy Birthday, Jesus. Your lottery number is 86!" Later at school I heard someone say that sign was sacrilegious and probably put up by some communists.

But you know something? I've got to admit I kind of liked that billboard. As a matter of fact, I really liked that billboard. Jesus cares about our spaced-out world and wants to be very much a part of it. And as His follower, I will not sit on the sidelines and watch this world race by me. I cannot day dream in front of color television letting commercials seduce me into buying things I don't need. As a Christian I am thrown full force into this maelstrom—in the middle of war, hunger, bigotry, and hatred. Why? Because I know who He is.

He's not a church and He's not an institution.
    He's a person.
He's not black or white, red or yellow.
    He's the Man who frees all men and women.
He's not a Democrat and He's not a Republican.
    He's the Lord of Heaven and earth.
He's not a capitalist or a communist.
    He's the Prince of Peace.
He's not a giant aspirin tablet for when life's a headache.
    He's the Way, the One Way, the only Way.
      You can go to a bottle or a pill for help

and only move a little closer to death.

You can make $20,000 a year but that won't
buy meaning and purpose for your
life.

You can tour the world and be just as
miserable in Paris as you were back
home.

Stop wasting time and money. Only the God who created you knows how to put you together again. He is the only one who can take the darkness of your life and turn it into light.

But remember. God doesn't grade on a curve. He won't let you slip into Heaven just because you walked down a sawdust trail at a revival meeting out of the chance that there might be a hell. He's not interested in how pious you can act, either. Or how many spiritual merit badges you can show off to the world. Men have stumbled down their "religious roads" for years only to find they were scrambling toward a DEAD END.

DEAD END

*There is a way which seems right to a
man, but its end is the way to death*
(Proverbs 14: 12 RSV).

I'LL NEVER FORGET that Sunday morning when I first
spotted him. There he sat, brooding in the next to the last
pew on the left side of the church. He looked so blue he
could spit ink.

This was sixth in a schedule of eight churches that our
group, the Good News Circle, was singing in. We were
all relieved to be playing at last to a congregation filled
with warm and obviously turned-on Christian people.
Some of them were clapping their hands with the music;
some were singing along with us; and everybody was having a great time in the Lord. Everybody, that is, except
him.

I decided to make this man with the glum countenance
my personal target. I looked directly at him during every
song; but the more we sang, the more he slumped. The
livelier the music got, the uglier he got. The more we
smiled, the more he scowled.

When the program was over, I jumped off the platform and ran down the aisle to get to him before he got away. I reached him at the back of the church and as I shook his hand I said, "Hi, I'm Bob. Isn't it great to be a Christian?"

He looked at me, grunted "Hummpf!" and briskly walked away. I could hardly wait to get to the seventh church.

Then I started thinking. "Hey, I've heard that 'hummpf' before. I guess I've known you longer than I thought, Grumpy." My mind flashed back to a Sunday morning when I was about twelve years old, watching the ushers receive the offering. I was alone in the middle of the pew and the usher had to walk all the way in with the offering plate. Just as he started to hand the plate to me, he tripped and the money went flying all over my lap, to the people in front of me, and on to the noisy floor below. I laughed so hard, I thought my sides would split! I thought that was the funniest thing I had ever seen. But then I looked directly into the eyes of the furious usher. He frowned down at me and said, "Hummpf! Bobbbyyy?!"

Did I ever feel terrible!

"I'm sorry, Grumpy.

I know I'm not as religious as the rest of the
people in the church.

Like old Brother Elmer over there.

Man, he knows all those big words like
resurrectify, sanctivacation, beget, begat,
and begut.

And I sure can't pray like the preacher.
My tongue gets all twisted on the
thee's, thou's and thuses.

I'm sorry, Grumpy."

That was the first time I felt I didn't belong in church. A couple of years later, it happened again. I was sitting in the back of the church with Jimmy, a friend of mine. Just as I was thinking the meeting was over, the pastor said, "And now, friends, we will celebrate the communion service together." That didn't particularly thrill me because I was eager to get home and play a little touch football before dinner. And besides, I didn't understand what this communion thing was all about anyway. But as a member of the church, I knew that I was expected to participate, and so I sat there waiting for the bread.

As I watched the deacons serving the congregation, I was trying to think of something that I could do that would make Jimmy laugh. By the time they reached us, I was ready. The deacon wasn't looking, so I took six or seven pieces of bread and stuffed them in my mouth. Oh, boy! I thought Jimmy was going to crack up. He was really impressed. Then when the grape juice came, it was his turn. He put the little glass up to the side of his mouth and poured the juice down his cheek and all over his white shirt. There was no way I could top that. My eyes filled with tears from trying to hold back the laughter.

IT'S BUMPY FOR GRUMPY

Then the worst happened. The preacher was reading from his Bible. But instead of looking at the Book he looked directly at me. Maybe no one else knew he was looking at me, but I felt the full force of his stare. What he was saying was meant for my ears: "If anyone eats this bread and drinks from this cup of the Lord in an unworthy manner, he is guilty of sin against the Body and Blood of the Lord."

Oh, that was it.

I knew I'd done an awful thing.

"Preacher, I'm sorry.

28

But I'm just a rotten little guy. I don't
belong here.

I'm not good enough to be a Christian."

I felt like a square peg in a round hole. I was certain I couldn't have been more out of place than I was in a church. As a kind of penance for the terrible things I had done in church, I secretly vowed never to bother Christians again.

I felt that way because I didn't understand what the church was all about. I thought it was a place where you went to learn how to be a Christian. But that's not even close.

When Hebrews 10:25 tells us to go to church, it doesn't mean that we should go so that we can get to know God; it means that we should worship with other brothers and sisters *because* we know God. Compared to many church strategies, this is a whole new ball game. It's especially good for the pastor, because finally he can stop trying to be what he was never supposed to be—a pursuer of sinners—and he can start being what he has always been commanded to be Biblically—a perfecter of saints. He can get someone else to drive the bus to pick up children for Sunday school, and spend that time studying his Bible. That way he can teach and nourish the flock that he is responsible for.

What a relief for your church when it can stop being a social club consisting of a few members that the minister talked into coming, and it can start being a football huddle where the team gets together as often as possible to talk over and pray about the game plan for that week. Then you break up and go out to pass the ball around. Christians who don't experience this often starve out their "faculty for fun" and find out all too soon that the grumpy road is the bumpy road.

Jesus said, "God is Spirit, and those who worship Him must worship Him in spirit and truth." This is tremendous news and explains why no tomb could contain the likes of our Lord. Since when do spirits have to use a door to go in or out? God's Spirit cannot be confined to four walls and a roof. We've got to stop trying to box Him in.

His church was never meant to be a shelter where Christians hide in the fellowship room, fearful that the world's fallout will contaminate their shining testimonies. Instead it is a launching pad from which Christians blast off in all directions, knowing that He will supply all the fuel our resurrected retro-rockets will ever need. And this is exactly how a communion service speaks to me now.

When Jesus took the bread and the cup and said, "Do this in remembrance of Me," He was telling us:

"Don't forget what I have done for you.

My blood covers your debt.

Accept my finished work on the Cross

and stop *trying* to be a Christian.

Jesus doesn't want our bargain basement religion.

He wants our lives.

The only sign that stands alongside a road of self-righteousness reads: DEAD END.

The bread during communion reminds me that Jesus said, "I am the Bread of Life . . . anyone eating this bread shall live forever." What a fantastic new covenant He has made with us. How can you be sullen with a promise like that? This is the source of our joy, that in Jesus we never die.

Now by joy I don't mean a joy-ride at the amusement park. The pressure to entertain and keep up with prime-time television is one of the biggest factors undercutting the church today. Instead of rugged, visionary believers, we're becoming better known as the "Presbyterian Ping-Pong Players," and "Baptist Bowlers and Bingo Buffs." Jesus must grow weary of looking for our fruits and finding only our denominational hang-ups growing from His vine.

What would men like Martin Luther, John Calvin, Pope Leo, and John Wesley say about this? No doubt they would say, "GET with Christ, and GO with Christ!" Jesus said, "By this shall all men know that you are My disciples, if you keep on showing love one to another." Love is an action word. It must be shown. It must be demonstrated. Read the description of a church that did exactly that:

> And all the believers met together constantly and shared everything with each other, selling their possessions and dividing with those in need. They worshiped together regularly at the Temple each day, met in small groups in homes for Communion, and shared their meals with great joy and thankfulness, praising God. The whole city was favorable to them, and each day God added to them all who were being saved (Acts 2: 44-47 LB).

SAVED, SATISFIED, AND PETRIFIED

I once talked with a pastor who told me that any resemblance between the Church described above and his parish would be "purely coincidental." He said, "If the Holy Spirit told us today that Jesus was coming back tomorrow, by the time we got a committee together and decided under which area the Rapture would come—missions, evangelism, finances, or transportation—and then waited for our monthly business meeting to act on it officially, we would have missed His coming by over forty days!"

I am convinced that the greatest obstacle to reaching this world for Jesus is the orthodox, professing, creed-proclaiming Christian who has at best the form of religion without its power (2 Timothy 3: 5), the Christian who says "I believe" and thinks that's enough.

Not long ago I found myself caught up in one of the most thrilling church meetings I've ever attended. I wasn't being stirred by beautiful music, or inspired by great preaching; I was simply listening to the impromptu testimonies of people in the congregation. Each participant could hardly wait for an opening so that he could tell something about how Jesus was working in his life.

As I left the gathering that night, I wondered why I hadn't seen more sharing times like this in the churches I'd visited. The answer quickly came to mind: there are a lot of churches who never allow for such a time in their programing because the people just don't have anything to share. It's hard to talk about your daily walk with Jesus when you have yet to take the first step.

There isn't time to waste. It does no good to meet in a church, talk a good fight, call ourselves a community of believers, and then speak in a stained-glass voice when the world cries out for help.

For too long we have been
    saved,
       satisfied,
          and petrified!
    Let's stop saying how much we love drunks
       Until we're ready to show the kind of compassion that sent Jesus into the bars of Jerusalem;
          Until we invite the poor guy into our home, and tell him about the Man who said,
             "I am the Living Water. He who drinks of

me will never thirst again" (John 4: 13).
Let's stop saying how much we love prostitutes,
fallen women, unwed mothers

Until we're ready to give evidence of the
kind of concern that drove Jesus into the flop-
houses around Palestine;

Until we tell that girl about the Man who
said,

"Woman, where are your accusers? Has no
man condemned you? Then neither do I.

Go, and sin no more" (John 8: 10, 11).

Let's stop saying how much we love Blacks, Whites,
Reds, Browns, and Yellows

Until we're ready to believe that all colors
are but different shades of God;

Until we invite that brother into our home,
and tell him about the Man who wrote the
real Emancipation Proclamation:

"If the Son sets you free, you will be
free indeed" (John 8: 36).

"Little children,

let us stop just *saying* we love people;

let us *really* love them,

and *show it* by our *actions*" (I John 3: 18
LB).

If these kinds of people have no place within the framework of our church or home, then neither does our
church or home have any place within the framework of
the Kingdom of God. The Church is not a supermarket
where we buy a half-pound of anything we want to believe in. It's a living organism, headed up by a Man who
says, "Go into all the world and preach the Gospel . . ."
(Mark 16: 15).

It's a well-known fact that it takes more muscles to

33

frown than to smile, so start smiling. There's a lot of work to be done, and you're going to need the extra energy!

I Love Mankind, It's Just the People I Can't Stand!

Well, now that you know Jesus says "go" how come you're still sitting there? Can't you make yourself love other people? You try, but you can't seem to do it, and you think that nothing could make you change?

With apologies to Eric Segal's *Love Story,* "Love *does* mean having to say you're sorry." Yes, even you, Christian, because there's no way you can give yourself to other people when *you* are constantly in the way. That's why the greatest need of the hour is good old-fashioned repentance; a turning around, a giving in to His way of love over our way of vanity and pride.

The Book of First John was written directly to Christians and yet I John 1: 8, 9 says that

If we say that we have no sin, we are only fooling ourselves, and refusing to accept the truth.

But if we confess [Love *does* mean having to say you're sorry!] our sins to him, he can be depended on to forgive us and to cleanse us from every wrong" (LB).

Jeremiah Was not a Bullfrog

It was a great day when God lifted up the prophet Isaiah. Here was a powerful messenger, ready to go anywhere to preach to the "heathen." But what did God do with him? He sent him right to his own people.

Later on, God called out a man named Jeremiah and burned a message of repentance into him so deeply that Jeremiah cried out with tears in his eyes, "His word is in my heart like a burning fire shut up in my bones!" But did God tell Jeremiah to take this fiery word to the wicked dregs of humanity? No! He made the prophet go and cry in the ears of Jerusalem. Now if there was ever a religious city in the world, it was Jerusalem; Jeremiah was told to begin right in the heart of God's own nation.

God didn't change the script for Ezekiel, either, when He sent him into the city. He said, "Begin at my sanctuary." God plays no favorites when it comes to obedience.

But do we really need to begin in our churches today? The following story answers that question for me.

THERE'S A SKELETON IN THE CLOSET!

"Hey Joyce! Someone's knocking at the door."

"I know, I've been listening. What time is it anyway?"

I looked at the clock. "It's 3:30! Honey, go get it, will you? I'll keep your side of the bed warm."

"No deal! I'm getting up earlier than you this morning. You get it."

"Oh, good grief!" I mumbled as I stumbled to the door. I couldn't have known how little sleep I would be getting for the next couple of days.

I opened the door and looked into the glazed eyes of a girl I'd met on a recent tour. Even though she was on downers which normally produce a depressed state, she was wild and almost frantic. Her T-shirt was drenched in blood and she firmly held a blood-stained knife in her right hand.

"Donna! Are you all right?"

There was no reply.

"Well, come on in!" I started to take her by the arm, but she weakly jerked away. She went over to the corner of our living room and sat down in a chair. I got a blanket and she wrapped it around her shoulders. Then I sat on the floor in front of her and waited.

Very slowly—because her scrambled mind was desperately trying to produce something logical—she told her story.

"Where were you tonight, Donna?"

"Somewhere in Chicago . . . lots of girls around . . . runaways . . . A fat blond and me . . . started playing a game . . . see who could make the littlest cut . . . She stuck me too hard . . . I got mad . . . stabbed her in the head . . . over and over . . . She's dead . . ."

As Donna started falling asleep, I took the knife from her, and Joyce put her to bed in the den. I notified the police and then left to search for the body.

As I was driving along, I started wondering how something like this could have happened. Her mother wasn't a prostitute. Her dad wasn't a junkie. She wasn't the victim of divorced parents. As a matter of fact, her father was superintendent of one of the largest Sunday schools in the area. And the parents of the girl who gave Donna the knife worked with the church youth group on Sunday nights.

I started to understand why God said, "Begin at My sanctuary." When the world looks at us Christians and says that it cannot believe in God, then we've got some changing to do.

TURN AROUND, TURN AROUND

Certainly God ordained the Church to go on forever, but what Church was He talking about? When Peter told Jesus that "You are the Christ, the Son of the living God," Jesus replied, "On this rock I will build my church, and the powers of death shall not prevail against it" (Matthew 16: 18 RSV). But when Jesus says, "On this rock . . ." He doesn't mean, "Upon the shoulder blades of Simon Peter will I build my Church." He is saying, "Upon this confession of Me as Lord will I build My Church and not even the powers of hell shall hold out against it."

As far as I'm concerned, Jesus' answer to Peter does not justify the existence of one brick church building in the country unless that building is constructed out of confessing disciples, believers who are actively involved in loving this world. And in order for some of us to reach this point, it's going to take some genuine turning around, some honesty that admits we haven't been quite as righteous as we thought. Consider what His Word tells us:

"I came not to call the righteous, but sinners" (Mark 2: 17 RSV).

"None is righteous, no, not one" (Romans 3: 10 RSV).

"When we put on our prized robes of righteousness we find they are but filthy rags" (Isaiah 64: 6 LB).

We discover that no one is good, no matter what kind of front we try to put on. When Jesus said, "I came not to call the righteous, but sinners," that must have been His subtle way of saying, "Some of you *good* people are so religious, you're pathetic! As long as you think you're first-rate, it does Me no good to summon you to salvation. And so I call to repentance those who admit they are sinners."

I don't know about you, but if there's any salvation going around, I want to be in on it. Sure, it might hurt my pride a lot to say "I'm sorry" and to admit I am human and need God's help to put my life together. But can you think of a better way to spend eternity than with Jesus?

A couple days after my wife gave birth to a great little guy, our son Christopher Paul, our pediatrician called her over to talk for a minute.

"I just wanted to warn you. When you get the baby home you can expect a few pretty rough weeks."

"Why's that, Doctor?"

"Well, my wife and I have a three-week-old baby. I come home from a hard day at the office knowing that she's had her hands full taking care of the baby. I walk in the door and she's crying and the baby's crying and then we all cry together. As I sit there in tears, I start thinking 'This can't be happening to me. I'm supposed to know how to handle these things. I'm a pediatrician.' "

With this same kind of truthfulness, you and I need to concede that even as professional Christians, we're still not gods. New life in the church begins with this new kind of honesty.

BRING BACK THE GOOD OLD DAYS

Nearly two thousand years ago, on the day of Pentecost, the very first local church came into existence. Over three thousand people were saved that day. Spirit-filled men assembled from every nation under Heaven. Their common bond was Jesus, and they could have cared less about differences in hair length, color of skin, or manner of speech. They hadn't learned to be sectarian yet. They were one Body, one Church. We can be like that congregation.

"We are all parts of one body, we have the same Spirit, and we have all been called to the same glorious future.

For us there is only one Lord, one faith, one

baptism, and we all have the same God and Father who is over us all and in us all, and living through every part of us" (Ephesians 4: 4-6 LB).

One of my favorite folksongs for several years has been "They'll Know We Are Christians by Our Love." Now it's time to be noticed by what we are letting God do through us.

"But when the Holy Spirit controls our lives he will produce this kind of fruit in us:

    love,

        joy,

            peace,

                patience,

                    kindness,

                        goodness,

faithfulness,

    gentleness,

        and self-control . . ."

            (Galatians 5: 22, 23 LB).

There is no end to the gifts of love that God has in store for us because there is no DEAD END to the path of a believer. It goes on for ever.

A bright new day is dawning for the real Church of Jesus, because more people are learning all the time that it just doesn't pay to be like Grumpy. Rather, they're starting to fit the description that James gave to those who travel on "God's narrow freeway," we call those happy . . . (James 5: 11 RSV). This happiness comes naturally when the next road sign is obeyed: YIELD.

YIELD

"The path of the godly leads to life. So why fear death?" (Proverbs 12: 28 LB).

It was almost 7:20 p.m. In just about ten minutes I was going to be married. "Fear" doesn't quite describe the state I was in. "Panic" comes a lot closer. My complexion was a chalky gray; my legs felt like rubber; I had shooting pains in my eyebrows. I was the big, brave groom.

My younger brother, Mike, doubling as my best man, was doing all he could to keep things under control.

"Just think," he volunteered out loud, "a few more minutes and my big brother bites the dust."

"Thanks a lot, Mike."

"No kidding, Bob, it's almost time. You'd better practice your vows one more time."

"Oh, all right. But I know them backwards and forwards."

At this point, let me give some heady advice to husbands-to-be: Don't try to memorize vows if they are longer than three words. A man may have a photographic memory, but if he's anything like the rest of us red-

41

blooded American chickens, when you see your beautiful bride coming down the aisle, your blood will turn to ice water. You won't remember your own name, and to play it safe, you'll just start saying "I do" every time the minister looks at you.

My own vows ran something like this: ". . . and in the presence of God and these witnesses, I pledge you my unalterable love and devotion, and promise to do my best to be the kind of husband the Bible declares to be right . . ."

I faced my brother, and for the last time, I began running through those all too familiar words: ". . . and in the presence of God and these witnesses, I pledge you my unalterable love and devotion, and promise to do my best . . . uh . . . uh . . . to do my duty . . . to God and my country . . . and to obey the Scout law."

I was horrified, but Mike was doubled over with laughter. Tears filled his eyes as he blurted, "I sure hope God's got a sense of humor, because this is going to be a *funny* wedding."

And it was.

But you know, I've got to agree with Mike. I sure hope God has a sense of humor too, because if He doesn't, I've certainly got Him pegged wrong. I believe that He is a God who loves a good laugh, and I'll bet Jesus had some terriffic times with His best friends, the disciples, just joking and laughing together.

It is impossible for me to picture this as a typical evening in the life of our Lord: Jesus and the disciples huddled around a blazing fire on a chilly winter evening; only Jesus is seated on one side of the fire and the disciples on the other, with the Master speaking in a sanctified voice, "Verily, verily, I say unto you . . ." This view is preposterous and dangerous. I can much more easily imagine the Carpenter and His friends traveling along the dusty old Jericho road toward Jerusalem, when Jesus, seeing that one of His disciples is in a cantankerous mood, begins walking along beside Him, and placing His hand on His companion's shoulder, says, "What's the matter, Matthew? Did you get out of the wrong side of the tent this morning?" And then, "Smile, my brother, Jesus loves you!"

If this sounds sacrilegious to you, then maybe you *need* your religion sacked. I want a faith that is alive and that brings me life. Whenever I played as a little boy, I never picked out the cemetery to play in. I never really enjoyed tiptoeing through the tombstones. You don't usually see long lines of people waiting to get into the funeral parlor on Saturday nights. Jesus said, "Follow me, and leave the dead to bury their own dead" (Matthew 8: 22 RSV). As new creations in Christ Jesus, we're supposed to concentrate on living, and yet, even our vocabulary is filled with sickness and death: "Oh, I'm just tickled to death,
thrilled to death,
starved to death,
worried to death,
scared to death,
I'm dead tired,
dead sure,
dead wrong,
dead on my feet,
and just dying to go!"

SAVE A FEW FOR WITCHY POO

God's house is definitely a place of worship, a special spot where we can go to spend a few moments just listening to Him. But it is also a place where laughter should

43

ring from its rafters. Christians have the only authentic and eternal reason for enjoying life, and there can't be anything wrong with enjoying it at church. Too often, the following situation holds true:

Li'l Johnny joins the Church
    and the long, bony fingers of Mrs. Witchy Poo
    and Mr. Crabby Appleton come darting out from
    behind a moldy pew
        pointing to a list of rules and regulations
        which will allow him to become religious.
But wait a second, Witchy!
    Hold the phone, Crabby!
        This is not your local city morgue.
            That boy just stepped through the door of a
            building that should be bubbling over
            with the love of Jesus.
                Didn't you know there's no law against
                having fun reading the Bible?
                    Stop holding your ascetic martyr-
                    dom up to God for Brownie points.
                    He's not impressed.
And one more thing, Mr. Appleton and Mrs. Poo.
    Stop spreading the rumor that Christianity is
    a religion of DO's and DON'T's.
        Christianity is not a religion, it's a
        relationship.
            When Johnny asks "Who is Jesus?" and you
            answer by saying:
                Don't do this!
                Don't touch that!
                Don't look at that!
                Don't go near that!
                    And for Heaven's sake,
                    Don't associate with *them!*

>   What can Johnny say but
>   Don't bother me!

Let's stop forbidding and start listening to Jesus saying
". . . and you will know the truth, and the truth
will make you free" (John 8: 32, RSV).

>   Jesus breaks the chains of hate and self-love
>   that tie us in knots.

>   He knocks down the prison walls that we
>   build around one another.

JESUS SIGNED MY PARDON

I know a man who understands firsthand what prison
walls are all about. He is serving a life sentence at a penal
institution in downstate Illinois, but you won't catch him
being bitter about it. He knows there are a lot of "fine
upstanding citizens" walking around outside who are
more imprisoned than he is. He has learned a valuable
lesson: Real freedom is an inside job; it happens within
a man, and only Jesus can free a man from himself. This
man, who may never again know what it is to take a walk
without a machine gun keeping track of him, wrote a
song that explains it all:

> I was in sin's prison, oh, so dark and cold,
> Just a lost sheep straying from God's eternal fold.
> But the door swung open, Jesus spoke to me,
> "I have signed your pardon, you may now go free."

> When my Savior led me from that awful place,
> I could hear the angels sing. They sang "Amazing
>   Grace."
> I knew that I was pardoned from all sin and shame.
> So then I joined the angels, Oh, glory to His
>   name!

> Life is now worth living, since I've been set free.

I'm glad He was willing to save a wretch like me.
Now I have a mansion, not a prison wall.
Jesus signed my pardon. Oh, yes, He paid it all.

Jesus signed my pardon, this I truly know.
Took my place at Calvary, now I don't have to go.
All my life I gave Him, He gave His life for me,
When He signed my pardon, there at Calvary.

I'm proclaiming what you are because of what Christ did: you're free! So keep looking up, Christian, and be happy. Why? Because Jesus is not our jailer, He's our *Savior*. He's not out to hurt our pride, He's out to kill it and to replace it with lasting liberty.

Jesus didn't come to count our Sunday school pins;
   He didn't come to slap us on the hands,
      and to make us sit up straight in the pew.
He didn't come to put us down,
   He came to take us up.
      He loves us!
         How much more can we ask?

CHIN-UPS ON THE GUTTER

Of all people, Christians have the right to be eternal optimists. But the way so many of us approach life—defeated and miserable—is downright criminal. We spend too much of our time reminding ourselves of how unworthy we are.

"Oh, I'm just no good.
   I'm undeserving.
      I'm a sinner."

God isn't impressed when we Christians tell Him how awful and terrible we are. Why? Because the Bible says: "We are his workmanship, created in Christ Jesus for good works" (Ephesians 2: 10 RSV). It's like telling your next door neighbor that you hate the house you just moved into, and hearing him reply, "I built that house!"

The Bible says that Jesus was made sickness and disease so that we can live in health (Isaiah 53: 6). What a dent that puts in our obsession with hypochondriasis. Instead of whining about our many ailments, we can claim the power of His promise (John 10: 10) and give the Great Physician a shot at our bodies.

For the Christian, living in health goes far beyond just feeling good physically. It also speaks of a healthy mind and attitude. All of life can be seen through pessimism or optimism.

Grumpy says:

"From the moment you are born into this world, you begin to die."

But Happy turns pessimism sunny-side up:

"From the moment you are born again, you begin to live for ever."

Grumpy wallows in his problems.

"Woe is me! If my name's not written in the Book of Life, my future home is the Lake of Fire." But Happy takes the high road:

"Praise the Lord! Because I know Jesus I have already passed from death to life."

To a Jesus person, all traffic lights are green. The apostle Paul sets this tone by spelling out exactly what God's will for our lives is:

"Rejoice always,
   pray constantly,
      give thanks in all circumstances;
         for this is the will of God in Christ Jesus
         for you" (I Thessalonians 5: 16-18 RSV).

47

Does that mean I've always got to be bubbling over with happiness, that I've always got to be smiling? Of course not. In fact, I'm very suspicious of anybody who's got the twenty-four-hour-a-day grin plastered on his face. It makes me wonder if he's a little bit put on and not quite genuine. When Paul said "Always be full of joy" he moved us back to the inside once again, where we discovered real freedom earlier.

Running on feelings alone kept me away from Jesus. I gauged the depth of my Christian life by the way I happened to feel at that moment. On four different occasions during my junior high and high school years I went forward when an evangelist gave an invitation to accept Christ. I was sincere each time and really wanted to become a Christian. I would cry and then feel absolutely wonderful for several hours. But when the tears dried there didn't seem to be anything left.

MISERY AT THE MOVIES

I got tired of this routine and by the time I left home for college I had resolved never to respond to an invitation again. However, in my sophomore year at the university a friend asked me to go downtown with him to see a show. I said "Sure!" having no idea he meant a "religious" movie. The film was Billy Graham's "The Restless Ones." I never had been moved so powerfully toward Christ as I was in that theater. I slouched down in my seat. I tried not to look at the screen. I tried to think about anything but Jesus. I was in agony and under conviction. My only relief was knowing we weren't in a church and that I could just walk out when the movie was over.

But no such luck. The movie ended, the lights came

on, and a man with a microphone stood in front of the screen to say, "If any of you wants to become a Christian, come to the front of the theater and we will talk and pray with you."

I knew I had to go down there. I'd always believed there was a God and that I needed to be closer to Him. Maybe now I could get there. I "went forward" again and a large man took me over to the side, got my name and address, and asked me why I had gotten out of my seat and had come to the front. I was so emotionally torn apart inside that I was simply no good at answering his questions and not much better at listening to what he had to say. All I remember is that poor guy with good intentions telling me as I walked away, "Keep trying, son."

I mulled that over all the way back to school: Keep trying. Keep trying.

"But mister! I've been *trying* all my life to get something going with God!"

By the time I reached my dormitory I knew that whatever had happened to me at the theater was gone.

"Dear God!
    Why doesn't it ever last?
        Are you some kind of supernatural tease?
            Will You just give me a touch of Your beauty,
                A taste of happiness,
                    and then pull it out of my reach?"

YIELD: THE RIGHT WAY

You've heard it said that "What you don't know won't hurt you," but that was hardly true in this case. What I didn't know was really hurting me, and I didn't discover it until I read Fritz Ridenour's book *How to Be a Chris-*

tian Without Being Religious. Because of this little book, I realized that God actually seeks me and I don't have to go looking for Him.

It's not a matter of me trying, it's a matter of Jesus' dying. God comes more than halfway down the road. He meets us on the common ground of his Son's death and Resurrection and tells us to stop trying. The road sign he raises to guide us is YIELD THE RIGHT WAY by which He is simply saying "Commit your way to Me. Trust in Me and I will act."

It's God's action, not ours:
> "But to all who received him,
>   who believed in his name,
>   he gave power to become children of
>   God" (John 1: 12 RSV).

God gives the power. Your salvation is His work!
> "And I am sure that God who began the good
>   work within you will keep right on helping you
>   grow in his grace
>   until his task within you is finally finished
>   on that day when Jesus Christ returns"
>   (Philippians 1: 6 LB).
>   When God starts something
>   you can be sure He'll finish it.
> "For God is at work within you,
>   helping you want to obey him,
>   and then helping you do what he wants"
>   (Philippians 2: 13 LB).

The reason I can rejoice always is that God is at work within me.

Since I have yielded to Him, I can say,
> "It is no longer I who live,
>   but Christ who lives
>   in me" (Galatians 2: 20 RSV).

With God on the inside, we can care less whether or not we always look happy on the outside. Don't worry anymore about not feeling like you're a Christian, and begin trusting His Word that if you really believe in Him, He will "never fail you nor forsake you" (Hebrews 13: 5 RSV) and you will ". . . know that you have eternal life" (I John 5: 13 RSV).

PRAY CONSTANTLY?

How can I always be praying? I go to church only twice a week!

When Paul said "Always keep on praying" (I Thessalonians 5: 17 LB) he meant that we can be in permanent touch with God. You can talk with Him when you're walking across campus, driving in your car, doing your laundry, or even when you're on a date. The best time that I find to talk to God is every morning in the shower. It's a good prayer place because the phone can't reach me, I can't hear the doorbell, and those few minutes of "shower power" clean up a lot more than just my body.

Why is it so easy, though, for us to spend hours talking to one another and only seconds with God? I've known guys and girls who can stay up all night "flapping their gums" at a pajama party or a fraternity bull session, but who doze off from exhaustion before they can say "Now I lay me down to sleep."

Could it be that Christians have simply lost the art of praying? While many churches are looking for better methods and plans to expand by, God is looking for better men and women of prayer. What the Church needs today is not more machinery or organization, but believers whom the Holy Spirit can use—children of prayer.

The disciples didn't ask Jesus to teach them to sing,

51

usher, or even perform miracles. Instead they asked Him, "Lord, teach us to pray" (Luke 11: 1 RSV).

GIVE THANKS IN ALL CIRCUMSTANCES?

Are you telling me that I've got to thank Him for things that go wrong, too?

The Bible says "We know that in everything God works for good with those who love him . . ." (Romans 8: 28 RSV). That's why you'll often see a guy who loves Jesus start smiling when something seemingly catastrophic has happened to him. He's not about to get an ulcer over anything that's in God's hands. He knows that both the good times and the bad times are God's time, and that it takes two mountains to make a valley.

It's amazing what this kind of positive attitude can do for your life. I heard of an old woman who had only two teeth left, one on top and one on the bottom. But instead of giving up and suffering from malnutrition, she rejoiced, saying, "Thank God they touch!"

PLEASE! CHOOSE SOMEONE ELSE

The Book of Job is an even better example of thanking God in spite of everything. Job was a good, God-fearing man with a large family and an even larger bank account. He was one of the wealthiest farmers in the entire country. One day he found himself in serious trouble. One by one he lost his oxen, cattle, sheep, and servants. As if that wasn't bad enough, a messenger came running to him and cried, "Your sons and daughters were eating at their brother's house when a terrible wind struck it and killed them as it fell!" When Job heard this, he tore off his shirt, shaved his head, fell on the ground and *worshiped* God, saying, "the Lord gave, and the Lord has taken away; blessed be the name of the Lord" (Job 1: 21 RSV).

Then one morning Job woke up covered from head to foot with sores and boils. No dermatologist could have cleared up those blemishes. His skin was no job for a sun lamp or a little skin cream. Job's body was one big boil. He was hurting so badly that his wife begged him to curse God and die.

That would have done it for me. If my wife had reached that point of desperation I would have thrown in the towel. Old Job could have reacted, "So I'm one of your *chosen* people? How about choosing someone else!" But instead he said to his wife, "Shall we receive good at the hand of God, and shall we not receive evil?" (Job 2: 10 RSV). Even in the middle of all his grief, Job found God near and cried out to Him. "I had heard of thee by the hearing of the ear, but now my eye sees thee" (Job 42: 5 RSV).

In the end the Lord blessed Job more than ever, giving him twice as much as he had before in possessions, friends, sons and daughters. You've got to expect great things when you start thanking God in spite of everything.

PRAISE THE LORD, ANYHOW

I was in the bedroom getting dressed when my wife very casually walked in and said, "I just had a wreck." She was so nonchalant that I thought she was kidding. Four years earlier she'd gotten in a wreck and had come home crying. She could see I didn't believe her so she repeated herself. "No kidding, honey, I just smashed our car, but the other driver is all right. A policeman came and took down the information and I told him it was all my fault."

"What? It was your fault," I choked, "and you're not even crying?" Then I started to catch on. Joyce and I had been trying to praise God for everything, no matter how terrible it seemed at the time. Believe me, that can be dynamite.

Later Joyce went to court expecting to pay a big fine, ready to accept any other penalty that came her way, and generally terrified at being in court for the first time in her life. But not only was she acquitted on all counts, but the court ruled that it was not her fault at all. Thank You Lord, in spite of everything!

And so we can
   rejoice always,
      pray constantly,
         give thanks in all circumstances,
           and be happy.

Because it's a fact, not just a feeling that God loves us. God did not send His Son into our world to condemn it but to save it. He didn't come to send us to hell, He came to love us to Heaven.

Certainly He is a just God and Jesus will some day come to "judge the living and the dead" (I Peter 4: 5), but the Bible tells us why Christ hasn't already come in judgment: "He isn't really being slow about his promised return, even though it sometimes seems that way. But he is waiting, for the good reason that he is not willing that any should perish, and he is giving more time for sinners to repent" (II Peter 3: 9 LB).

God really doesn't want any of us to die. In fact, He is waiting while we decide whether or not we want to live. God loves us. It's barely conceivable, but it's true.

Now I can sing "Oh, how I Love Jesus."
  Why?
     Because He first *scared* me? No!

Because He first loved me!

Love is the anchor, the bedrock of Christianity. It cost a Man his life. I am sobered by the thought of the Cross. Jesus didn't want to make the trip to Calvary. He was in ". . . such agony of spirit that he broke into a sweat of blood, with great drops falling to the ground as he prayed more and more earnestly" (Luke 22: 44 LB).

Later He set the same requirements for us when He said that if we wanted to be His followers we would have to deny ourselves and take up our own individual crosses.

WHAT A WAY TO GO

But you say, "I thought we were talking about being happy. What's all this about death and crosses?"

Don't you see?

This is the whole point.

Christians plant crosses on top of their
churches because they believe in death.

Even a good man dies.

Even a physician dies.

Even a wonderful teacher dies.

Even a guy in his thirties dies.

Even Jesus died.

He was all these things and more.

He proved beyond doubt that the planet
Earth is a whirling cemetery.

That everyone dies down here.

Even God's Son.

Sure, we can take His Cross and carve it up into
guitars, and baseball bats,
surfboards and Ping-Pong paddles,
and bleacher seats,

                    but it remains
                        the Cross.
        It still cries out that the roar of the crowd
            will never silence death.
                Death is our powerful enemy and we try to put
                it off with every meager tool we can lay our hands
                on.
                    We fight it with
                        heart transplants,
                            cobalt treatments,
                                and insulin shots.
                    We fight its signs of old age with
                        mud packs,
                            cold creams,
                                and wigs.
                    But even more certain than taxes
                        our arteries harden,
                            our joints calcify,
                                our hearts stop.
        But the reason we can be happy is that the closer we
        come to the Cross, the better we can hear Jesus shout, "It
        is finished!" What is finished? Death!
            The grave couldn't hold Him even a full weekend.
                He burst out of His tomb,
                    walked through closed doors without knock-
                    ing, and
                        made a believer out of doubting Thomas.
                        He appeared to 500 people at one time
                        proving that what happened to
                                Martin Luther King, Jr.,
                                Jimi Hendrix
                                John F. Kennedy
                                Bobby Kennedy,
                                Janis Joplin,

                    the Israelis at Munich,
                    two of my aunts, and
                    one of my grandparents,
                    is on its way out.
    "O death, where then your victory?
        Where then your sting?" (I Corinthians 15: 55 LB).
        So let's sing Handel's *Messiah,*
            And let's sing *Oh Happy Day,*
                because Jesus says,
                    "I'm alive, and death is on its way
                    out!"

YOU CAN'T KILL A DEAD MAN

This is exactly why a Christian funeral should be a cele-
bration. By the way, all of you are invited to my funeral.
But let me warn you right now: don't cry at my casket. I
like where I'm going. And so you'll never catch me com-
plaining about my work, because you certainly can't beat
the "retirement plan." Besides, don't you know you can't
kill a dead man? That's exactly what I became when I
started walking with Jesus. Galatians 2: 20 says, "I am
crucified with Christ." Now you can understand why the
early believers turned the world upside down for the
Lord. No power in the world can withstand an army of
dead men. Before Jesus sent His disciples out, He gave
them the key to victory by saying, "Don't be afraid of
those who can kill only your bodies—but can't touch your
souls! Fear only God who can destroy both soul and body
in hell" (Matthew 10: 28 LB).
    Those Christians had the Romans running scared be-
cause their swords could stop only the Christians' bodies,
not their spirits. Nero couldn't figure out why they weren't
afraid to die. What he didn't understand was that they

were already dead. And so Rome fell and people started naming their dogs "Nero" and their children "Paul."

It was Paul who said: "Living or dying we follow the Lord. Either way we are his" (Romans 14: 8 LB).

Can you imagine anyone actually being happy to die? It was said of a spunky, old retired minister named Henry Venn, after being told that he was dying, ". . . the prospect made him so jubilant and highspirited that his doctor said that his joy at dying kept him alive a further fortnight." With his last breath, he might easily have been heard saying, "What a way to go!"

OPEN THE DOOR

By now you must realize why I have very little patience with down-in-the-mouth Christians. When even death has no hold on us, we have a responsibility to be filled with hopefulness, enthusiasm, and confidence in the future. As a follower of Jesus Christ I don't cheat death, I beat death. That's why I just can't comprehend negative brothers and sisters who sit around all the time saying "Well, if God wants me to do something, He'll open all the doors." Or, "If it's the Lord's will, it will just happen." Where does this pitiful approach leave you when someone walks into your office or home and announces that he is contemplating suicide? What will be your reply? ". . . Uh, well, if it's the Lord's will, go ahead. It won't hurt much?" There are certain spiritual truths for which we need no doors of confirmation to open. The Bible says that God "is not willing that any should perish . . ." (II Peter 3: 9 LB).

Stop making God your scapegoat. It does no good to tell yourself that "If it's the Lord's will," you will get up and turn off your television set, and your front door will miraculously open, and you will go over to your next door neighbor's, turn off his television set, and finally share God's plan of salvation for his life. There are certain Biblical imperatives we cannot avoid. One such charge is directly from Jesus: "As the Father has sent me, even so I send you" (John 20: 21 RSV). An obvious response to this point is, "But, Bob, that's easy for Jesus to say. He's the Son of God!"

Well, who do you think you are, Christian? Romans 8: 16, "For his Holy Spirit speaks to us deep in our hearts, and tells us that we really are God's children" (LB). We are God's children; His sons and daughters. Therefore, we can confidently and joyfully share His love with other potential family members.

The apostle Paul was a man who never waited for a door to just open somewhere. Instead, with God's Word in his mind and heart, he kicked the doors down. As Paul said,

"So I run straight to the goal
   with purpose in every step.
      I fight to win" (I Corinthians 9: 26 LB).
"I can do all things in him
   who strengthens me" (Philippians 4: 13 RSV).

Paul could make fantastic statements like these because he personally knew the God who says, ". . . nothing will be impossible to you" (Matthew 17: 20 RSV).

Your retort this time might be, "That's all right for Paul, he's an apostle!"

Once again, who do you think you are, Christian? You share one great common denominator with apostle Paul: You are both believers, and as such you might as well claim what is already yours—the fantastic promise of Jesus held within John 14: 12, 13:

"In solemn truth I tell you, anyone believing in me shall do the same miracles I have done, and even greater ones, because I am going to be with the Father. You can ask him for *anything,* using my name, and I will do it . . ." (LB).

If this is not a call to happiness, nothing is. You just can't stay grumpy for long in the mountain-moving atmosphere that Jesus creates.

A MILLION TICKETS

But you know, even though I've walked His road for several years now, it's sometimes difficult for me even yet to understand how the Creator can love His creation so much. This thought hit me like a ton of bricks one night after the Good News Circle had just finished a Jesus rally. One of the guys in the group went out to get his car and came back for the rest of us. Though usually a pretty level-headed person, he just wasn't with it that night. He must have been thinking about what a great time he'd just had with Jesus, because he certainly wasn't thinking about driving.

There he was, driving the wrong way down a one-way street, little knowing that in the shadows of the roadside a policeman watched every move he made. And did he ever make some moves! He almost ran another car off the road, and, as if that weren't enough, he ran a red light.

In no time the officer pulled him over and slowly walked to the car, his head shaking in disbelief. Butch (thanking God in spite of everything) rolled down his window and faced the officer.

"Okay, buddy, let me see your driver's license."

Butch felt his back pocket . . . front pocket . . . shirt pocket . . . pants cuffs . . . "Oh, officer? I . . . uh . . .

guess I don't . . . uh . . . have my license with me."

"What! Don't you know that I could give you a million tickets for what you've done tonight? But go ahead . . . you can leave . . . you're free."

Butch came right back and told me the whole story. We both immediately thought the same thing: Jesus also could say,

For what you have done,
>I could write you a million tickets!
>>But because I love you,
>>>I'll take the blame.
>>>>You're free!
>>>>>Now you can be really happy!

"For God was in Christ,
>restoring the world to himself,
>>no longer counting men's sins against them
>>but blotting them out.
This is the wonderful message
>he has given us to tell others" (II Corinthians 5: 19 LB).

So let's tell them!
>Let's shout it from the mountaintop!
>>We want our world to know!
>>>The Lord of love has come to us!
>>>>We want to pass it on!
>>>>>Let's GO!

GO

And the master said to the servant, "Go out to the highways and hedges, and compel people to come in, that my house may be filled" (Luke 14: 23 RSV).

NEAR THE END of my senior year at seminary, I was sitting in a hallway chair of a large church, nervously waiting to be called to a room down the hall. I was about to face the Ordination Council, twelve ministers who had the authority to bar me from the ministry or to approve my requirements for ordination. How I wanted to impress them! After all, twenty years of education weighed in the balance. To add to the tension, it suddenly hit me that my academic career was almost over and now I had to go out and *work* for a living.

The longer I sat there the more paranoid I became. "What's taking them so long? Why don't they just drill me and get it over with? What kind of questions are they going to ask anyway?" With a written exam you can get your thoughts together first and then set them down in an orderly fashion. A written exam is usually on classroom theory anyway. But getting the second degree from a bunch of guys who are out in the field working in the "real" world—well, that was something I wasn't sure I could handle. I frantically paged through Paul Little's *Know What You Believe* as if that would somehow get me through the next couple of hours.

BRING ON THE LIONS!

I was far from feeling spiritual (the thought of praying had not even crossed my mind), but what was about to happen to me could only have been planned from above. As I sat glowering at my book, my peripheral vision picked up a small figure approaching from the right. I looked up to see a three or four-year-old girl who had wandered away from the other children in the church's day care center. I quickly looked down again, hoping she would walk on by. Instead, she boldly marched up to me and lisped, "Mithster. Hey mithster!"

I tried to act tough. "Go 'way, kid. I'm studying."

But she wouldn't give up. "Hey mithster. Mithster!"

I could tell she wasn't going to let me alone until I listened to her, and she was so cute I finally said, "What do you want?"

She pointed to something behind me and asked, "Hey mithster, who's that?"

I turned around and saw, hanging over the drinking fountain, the most beautiful picture of Jesus I had ever seen. "Why, that's Jesus, honey."

She looked at the picture for a long time and finally sighed, "Oh. Jethuth."

I melted. This little angel by the name of Darcy taught me in three minutes more than a lot of us learn in three years of seminary. She shamed me into realizing the whole reason I was there, the entire purpose in my seeking ordination: Jesus. I gave her a big hug, thanked God for the swift kick, and pledged that I would spend the rest of my life telling people who the man in that picture is: "He's Jethuth!"

Bring on that Ordination Council!

Bring on the Sanhedrin!

Bring on the lions!

I was ready for anything. I didn't care if I was refused ordination; I knew that nothing was going to stop me from pointing to the Cross. I wasn't going to be bashful anymore.

As it was, those twelve men were very warm and receptive. We had a great time talking about Jesus, and Darcy!

STRONGER THAN DIRT

You might say to me, "Go ahead and talk to people about Jesus all you want, but I believe a man's religion is a very personal matter. It's his own business and we should never discuss it."

I appreciate your sensitivity more than your theology, however. Consider the following story that was reported in *Campus Life* magazine several years ago:

A well-dressed young woman, sight-seeing in New York City slums, became upset over a dirty ragamuffin playing in the filth of the gutter.

"Look at that child!" she cried, "Why doesn't someone clean it up? Where is its mother?"

"Well," explained the guide, "it's this way, Miss. The child's mother loves her child, but she doesn't hate the dirt. You hate the dirt, but you don't love the child. Until love for the child and hate for the dirt get into the same heart, the poor child will remain just about the way it is."

This is exactly why Christ came into the world. His heart contained love for the sinner, yet hatred for the sin. And Jesus alone gives power over that sin. Therefore, Jesus said, "I have been given all authority in heaven and earth" (Matthew 28: 18 LB).

II Timothy 1: 7 reminds us that "God did not give us a spirit of timidity but a spirit of power and love and self-control" (RSV). As His followers, only we can get "love for the child" and "hate for the dirt" into the same body. Therefore we can do more than sight-see; we can point that person to the "redemption center"—the Cross.

THE MEANS TO A BEGINNING

But you could also say, "I don't like 'Bible-beaters' to force their religious views down the throats of everyone they meet."

Let me remind you that we Christians don't witness to our faith just because we want to or even because we enjoy doing it; we witness because He tells us to. We follow His imperative to

"Go therefore

and make disciples of all nations . . .

teaching them to observe

all that I have commanded you" (Mat-

thew 28: 19, 20 RSV).

When others block our way with STOP signs, we look higher to God's GO sign because the Bible says that we believers are Christ's ambassadors (II Corinthians 5: 20). An ambassador is one who represents the ruler or king, and as ambassadors of Christ, we represent the King of kings (Revelation 19: 16). Psalm 107: 2 declares, "Let the redeemed of the Lord say so"; not just "act so," but *say* so.

66

Besides, when you love Jesus, you can't keep from telling others about Him. I agree with Paul who says, ". . . the love of Christ controls us" (II Corinthians 5: 14 RSV), or as the New English Bible translates it, ". . . the love of Christ leaves us no choice."

I witness because it's my responsibility (Matthew 28: 19), because the love of Christ leaves me no choice, and because I like the results seen in II Corinthians 5: 15:

"He died for all, that those who live
    might live no longer for themselves but
        for him who for their sake died and was raised"
            (RSV).

Witnessing is often the means to a beginning for many lost people. Seeing the power of Jesus change their lives has become my steady vision and constant goal. But the greatest "goal-chaser" of all time was Paul who said in Philippians 3: 13, 14:

"Forgetting the past and
    looking forward to what lies ahead,
        I strain to reach the end of the race
            and receive the prize for which God
                is calling us up to heaven
                    because of what Christ Jesus
                        did for us" (LB).

Paul's vision was alive and active. He was always reaching out and would not stop, because he knew that when vision disappears, evangelism dies. "Where there is no vision, the people perish" (Proverbs 29: 18 KJV).

Explo '72 with almost 100,000 Christians gathered together for a week in Dallas, was one of the greatest experiences of my life. It was there I heard that the three greatest abilities you could ever have are: *avail*ability, *expend*ability, and *adapt*ability. I've thought a great deal about this and believe that only a strong vision of who

Jesus can be in your life can give you these "abilities."

A fantastic story unfolds in the eighth chapter of Acts. Philip was holding a very successful "revival" over in Samaria when God said to him, "Leave your big meeting and go to the desert to talk to a man." What would your reply be if you had been Philip?

"But Lord! The whole city of Samaria is listening to me and the offerings have been just great!"

But God said "Go" and Philip went.

He found himself in the middle of the Gaza desert looking for a man he'd never seen before. Soon enough, Philip saw an Ethiopian poring over the book of Isaiah. Philip must have thought, "Something strange is going on." Then God told him to go over and walk beside the chariot. Now Philip *knew* something strange was going on. He could have called the whole thing off right there by saying,

"Forget it.

   This is getting ridiculous.

      I don't even speak Ethiopian.

         Besides, a man's religion is a per-
         sonal matter."

But not Philip. He *ran* to the chariot and asked the guy if he understood the passage he was reading. The man said, "How can I when there is no one to instruct me?" Then he begged Philip to come into the chariot and teach him. Philip climbed in and beginning with this same Scripture, used many others to tell him about Jesus.

What were the results of this young believer taking time out to share his faith? The Bible states that,

"As they went along the road they came to some water

68

and the eunuch said, 'See, here is water! What is to prevent my being baptized?'

"And Philip said, 'If you believe with all your heart, you may.'

"And he replied, 'I believe that Jesus Christ is the Son of God.' And he commanded the chariot to stop, and they both went down into the water, Philip and the eunuch, and he baptized him" (Acts 8: 36-38 RSV).

I think God taught Philip two very important things in this wonderful happening:

1. Look what can happen when you make yourself available to Me.

2. Look what can happen in one-to-one sharing.

Mass evangelism is important and definitely Biblical when it's done with God's stamp on it, but just think about the potential of one-to-one sharing. Let's say through the evangelistic ministry of the Good News Circle, God continues to convert about 5,000 people a year. At the end of thirty-two years that would be 160,000 souls won for Christ. That's just great, huh? But wait a minute; before somebody hangs another Sunday school pin on us, grasp the following statistics. If in this coming year just one person becomes a Christian, and I spend the entire twelve months with that person, teaching him and growing with him; and if the two of us go out and each find another person to share with for the next year; and if the four of us then go out, and so on, then by the end of thirty-two-years three billion people would know eternal life in Jesus! It's almost enough to make me unpack my suitcase, sell my guitar, and stay home . . . almost.

"The harvest is so great,
   and the workers are so few," he told his
   disciples.

69

>   "So pray to the one in charge of the harvest-
>   ing,
>
>>   and ask him to recruit more workers
>>   for his harvest fields" (Matthew 9:
>>   37, 38 LB).
>
> Okay, Lord!
>   I'm praying and asking.
>   Send us more workers!
> There are vast fields of human souls
>   ripening all around us;
>   they are ready now for reaping.
> Lord, help us make ourselves more *available* to You.

EXPENDABILITY

Webster's dictionary says that if you are expendable
you are ". . . worth sacrificing to gain an objective." For
instance, Abraham was ready to kill his own young son
in order to prove that God was first in his life. Now that's
expendability. Abraham was 100 years old; his wife,
Sarah, was ninety; and Isaac was their only son. The old
fellow knew that he wasn't going to have many more children. But because he obeyed God, the Lord not only saved
the boy but made this promise to Abraham:

> "I will bless you with incredible blessings and multi-
> ply your descendents into countless thousands and mil-
> lions, like the stars in the sky, and the sand along the
> seashore."

King Nebuchadnezzar built a golden idol ninety feet
tall and ordered everyone to fall down on his knees and
worship the statue whenever the "band" started to play. If
he refused, the fiery furnace would be his next stop.
No one refused. That is, no one but three young believers
named Shadrach, Meshach, and Abednego. The king had

the boys brought before him and said,

"You guys have one more chance.

When the band strikes up,

when the flute toots,

you'd better make dust fly, boys.

If you don't bow down,

you'll burn in my fiery furnace,

and what god can deliver you then?"

With great boldness, our three young friends stated very matter-of-factly,

"Our God could easily deliver us

from your fire, O King,

but even if He doesn't,

we could never worship that hunk

of junk."

The Bible tells us that the king was so filled with fury that his face became dark with anger. He ordered his furnace heated seven times hotter than ever before, and commanded his strongest soldiers to tie up the prisoners and throw them into the fire. The flames were so intense that they consumed the king's men as they hurled the boys in!

And so Shadrach, Meshach, and Abednego fell down, bound, into the roaring blaze. But King Nebuchadnezzar jumped up like he'd seen a ghost and asked his servants how many men he had thrown into the fire. They answered, "Just three, sir." And the King said,

"But I see four men loose,

walking in the midst of the fire,

and they are not hurt;

and the appearance of the fourth is like

a son of the gods" (Daniel 3: 25 RSV).

That's who He should look like, king: He *is* God. The Lord takes care of His own, so don't be surprised that the fire didn't touch Shadrach, Meshach, and Abednego; that their coats weren't scorched, and that they didn't even smell like smoke.

God lived through them in that furnace because they were ready to die for Him in there. They were willing to be sacrificed to gain an objective: that everyone who saw them refuse to bow to the idol would know that they worshiped a God of love and not scrap metal. They believed in Him, and as far as they were concerned, after walking with the living God for awhile, everything else was just toothpaste. They practiced expendability for their faith and God took care of them.

A lot of well-intentioned people take a stand for Jesus, but then just keep standing there. We need to practice expendability with a new spiritual consciousness, not caring how much self-glory we can attain as we join this socially-active Jesus movement. Our Lord has never been all that interested in "joiners" anyway. You can get just about anyone to join just about anything if you give them a red button, a 25¢ certificate, and a bumper sticker. But Jesus doesn't want joiners. He wants disciples.

ADAPTABILITY

In Acts 10: 20 God tells Peter to do something that I don't think the old fisherman was very excited about doing. His orders were to visit Cornelius, the Roman. Peter didn't want to go because it was against the law for a well-bred Jew to enter the home of a Gentile. He wanted to pull an "Archie Bunker," but God told him to forget his bigotry and get over to Cornelius' house and adapt.

Jesus said you can't put new wine in old wineskins. They will burst. Neither can you put the new vision of today's Christian into the old structures of yesterday's Chris-

72

tianity. You don't have to worry about the *message* changing, because the content is Jesus and He ". . . is the same yesterday and today and for ever" (Hebrews 13: 8 RSV). But the *method* must continue to change as God directs.

In his book, *The Church at the End of the Twentieth Century,* Frances Schaeffer reveals that there are actually very few norms commanded by God for the New Testament form of the Church. He states,

". . . there are vast areas which are left free. There is form and there is freedom . . . anything the New Testament does not *command* in regard to church form is a freedom to be exercised under the leadership of the Holy Spirit for that particular time and place."

Even though this thinking may be revolutionary, it shouldn't trouble any of us who love Jesus and want to see the world won over to Him. What's wrong with seeing guys and girls gathered on the carpet at the front of the sanctuary instead of sitting straight-laced in a pew near the back? Besides it's easier to get on your knees when you're already on the floor!

YOU'RE ALL HEART, PAUL

I have greedy spells when I almost covet the great heart of the apostle Paul. Reread I Corinthians 9: 19-23. His compassion is almost unbelievable. In those passages, Paul says, "I have become all things to all men, that I might by all means save some." He would risk anything to introduce people to Jesus. Once he said, "I would be willing to be forever damned if that would save you" (Romans 9: 3 LB).

Paul's words speak loudly enough, but his actions speak even louder. Because he was always *available,* ready to *expend* himself at any time, and more than willing to *adapt* for Jesus, Paul was five times given the terrible thirty-nine lashes of the Jews, three times beaten with rods, three times shipwrecked, and once made the target of every rock the Jews could get their hands on, and on . . . and on . . . (II Corinthians 11: 23-29). Finally he was beheaded outside of Rome.

But in his own words, "For me to live is Christ, and to die is gain" (Philippians 1: 21 RSV). Paul gave his life because he believed and cared. Why is it that so many of us say we believe but don't act as if we care? Do we really believe that people who aren't with Jesus are eternally lost? Or is hell a concept that went out with the Dark Ages? My Bible still reads that hell is a viable option for anyone who wants it. And what's even more alarming is that you don't have to do anything to be lost. You don't have to curse God or join the nearest witches' coven or smoke cigars to rate eternal death. All you have to do is be outside of Jesus: "He who has the Son has life; he who has not the Son has not life" (I John 5: 12 RSV).

Now, do you see why we cannot afford to be bashful?

I Can't Come out to Play Anymore

If a major bottling company here in America can call a meeting of its board of directors and vow that before the end of the decade, every person in the world would have had the opportunity to taste its product;

If communism can pledge its every energy to bury my children under a Godless regime;

If all you have to do to get in touch with atheist Madeline Murray-O'Hare is address the envelope, Atheist: Houston, Texas;

Then it only makes sense that I'm going to spend all the time I've got giving people the opportunity to find out how Jesus can give new life.

God never told the world to go to church: He told the church to go to the world. According to the late Martin Luther King, Jr., if we don't tell people about Jesus, we are keeping Him on the Cross. And Paul said, "How can they hear about him unless someone tells them?" (Romans 10: 14 LB).

Jesus' message cuts through facades and plastic barriers like a two-edged sword, and brings life where death and deceit have stalked. As His witness, I want to see living beings, living creations from the hand of God. I want to see little children, moms and dads, grandmas and grandpas who are alive. I long to look upon the land of the living, not the creations of the dead; the homes of the Holy Spirit, not the tombs of the past. I want to touch and warm, and win the souls of men to Jesus.

Let the dead bury their own dead. Let the dead go sight-seeing in the mausoleums of men. But as for me and my house, we will live in the land of the living God.

"What I tell you now in the gloom,
  shout abroad when daybreak comes.
    What I whisper in your ears,
      proclaim from the housetops!"
        (Matthew 10: 27 LB).

The road sign clearly reads GO, just as Jesus said "Go out to the highways." But as we yield the right way and begin to go out onto the highway of life, we find that we need instruction on how to MERGE with other traffic. Read on.

MERGING TRAFFIC

So take a new grip with your tired hands,
stand firm on your shaky legs, and mark
out a straight, smooth path for your feet
so that those who follow you, though
weak and lame, will not fall and hurt
themselves, but become strong (Hebrews
12: 12, 13 LB).

IN THE SPRING of my second year of college, I started
suffering from a condition known as acute conjunctivitis.
My eyes were messed up and nobody knew why. The doctor told me it was some kind of allergy and he was going
to track down the source. I told him, "Fine, but wait until after final exams so I'll have an excuse not to take
them."

I wasn't too excited about the idea, but I figured that
an allergy test must be pretty harmless anyway. I thought
they'd probably give me an aspirin, check my pulse, and
let me go back to school. At least that's what I thought.

Let me give you some advice: Don't ever be allergic
to anything. And whatever you do, don't allow anyone to
talk you into taking an allergy test. It was akin to some

kind of weird Chinese torture. I thought they were going to pound bamboo shoots under my fingernails next. One by one the doctor put one hundred and fifty needle scratches on my back. The sweat poured down my arms as I sat tensely on the edge of the operating table. By the time he had reached one hundred I started saying "Ouch!" before he even touched me.

Worst of all, the results showed I was allergic to something that had nothing to do with my eye trouble: spinach! I vowed to never watch another Popeye cartoon.

I told one of my fraternity brothers about the whole thing and I have never forgotten his reaction: "How can you be allergic to something that's good for you, Laurent?" Even though I knew he was kidding, I took him very seriously.

ALLERGIC TO JESUS

One evening several years later, as we were finishing up a Jesus rally, my friend's words came back to me. A girl had come to me and said, "There's a guy up in the bleachers who's really mad at you." She proceeded to tell me his name and where I could reach him that night. I decided to find out what it was all about. He lived in a cabin quite a distance from town, and it took me a while to find it. It was nearly 2 a.m. by the time I got to his place, but he wasn't asleep and he really wanted to talk. I was immediately impressed with him; he was a sharp looking guy and had personality-plus. But his first words knocked me off my seat: "I just wanted you to know that I've hated you and your group from the minute you came to town. You make me sick!"

I mean, people have subtly tried to let me know when they haven't liked one of the songs we did, or if they didn't agree with something I said, but this guy had a whole new approach.

He explained how he became more miserable with each of our meetings; how he became physically sick as he sat and listened to us. He said he couldn't wait until we left. The more I listened the more I understood what he was saying: he was under conviction. God was speaking to him and he was doing everything he could to not listen. That's why he got sick when he heard me talk about Jesus. He was allergic to something that was good for him: Jesus. I explained this to him, and he got so excited about knowing what was wrong with him that he prayed to receive Christ right there on the spot. Praise, God, he's not sick anymore.

In the last chapter we learned that Jesus commands us to go into the world to spread the good news of His love. But the really difficult task is to learn how to merge with the traffic of the world and lead people onto the one-way road of eternal life. How do you get people to listen? How do we witness? These next few pages are devoted to helping you do just that. They won't show you how to become a soul-winner in four easy lessons, or how to notch another victim on the handle of your evangelistic six-shooter. But they might help you understand what it means to be a witness.

As a matter of Fact

Let's see if Dan Webster can help us again. He says that witnessing is "an attesting of a fact." The fact of Jesus Christ is the biggest advantage we've got going for us as God's witnesses. I discovered in seminary, much to my delight, that there are tremendous proofs for the authenticity of the Bible, that you don't have to assassinate your brains in order to follow Jesus, and that Christianity is a rational philosophy of life. I am commanded to love God with my mind as well as my heart and soul (Mark 12: 30).

In his book, *Set Forth Your Case,* Clark Pinnock states "that the Gospel rests upon an objective historical foundation is a priceless asset in this world in which there is a cafeteria of clues as to the meaning of the universe. The basis on which we rest our defense of the Gospel consists of evidence open to all investigators. The non-Christian has no right to disregard the Gospel because it is a matter of 'faith' in the modern sense. On the contrary, it is a matter of fact."

It is a sad commentary on contemporary evangelical Christianity, that while the world cries out for help, we who have the answers hide behind walls of ignorance. If the Good News is not a fairy tale, then let's start passing it on as an intelligent faith.

WHO'S GOT THE BODY?

In the New Testament, Jesus repeatedly points to the Resurrection as the ultimate sign of His authenticity (John 2: 18-21). We have the written evidence from six witnesses—Matthew, Mark, Luke, John, Paul, and Peter —that Christ was raised from the dead. Some of the written record is dated within ten years of the Resurrection.

John F. Kennedy died on November 22, 1963. Can you imagine the reception one would get if he ran into the streets now proclaiming that JFK was the Son of God? He would be quickly ushered to the nearest padded cell. Why? Because there are millions of people alive today who are close enough to the events of 1963 to know for certain that the late president was not the Christ. In the same way, the writings and claims of those six witnesses would have been stopped immediately if they had not been true. There were plenty of people who would have loved to stop them. You must remember that Christianity was born and developed in a pagan, Roman culture that was violently opposed to it. But the records of the apostles had to be accepted as eyewitness accounts. I Corinthians 15: 4-8 contains a list of those who actually saw Christ alive after his death.

But couldn't the disciples have stolen the body and pretended that Jesus had risen? If that were so, what would you do with the Roman guard and the sealed tomb? Besides, why would the same disciples who ran away terrified and denied Jesus the night He was arrested, suddenly do an about-face and die martyrs' deaths over belief in a Resurrection that was a lie?

But couldn't the Jewish or Roman leaders have moved the body? If that were true, why didn't they produce the body and put a quick end to all the preaching about the Resurrection? Instead they had to be satisfied with persecuting the early Church, and walking up and down the streets of Jerusalem, Ephesus, and Rome, crying, "Who's got the body?"

The fact is there wasn't any body. Jesus had gone to be with the Father (John 14: 12).

In light of the overwhelming evidence for the Christian claims, the apostle Paul told King Agrippa that he had no excuse for remaining an agnostic ". . . for I am persuaded that none of these things has escaped his notice, for this was not done in a corner" (Acts 26: 26 RSV). Acts 1: 3 says that Jesus presented himself alive after His Crucifixion with many "infallible proofs."

Jesus Christ was a public figure,

And His Resurrection was a public event.

Now go make His Good News public.
But before you "merge,"
keep the following important points
in mind.

BE PREPARED

Do you guys remember the first time you kissed a girl? Well, I do. I planned for months ahead. I wanted to make sure I was a good kisser so I practiced. I kissed everything in sight, and when my big chance came, I was prepared. The fact that the poor girl hated it didn't phase me. I knew there would be other opportunities and I would be ready.

If it means so much to us to be prepared for just about everything else, why won't we be equally equipped to witness? Peter says, "Always be prepared to make a defense to any one who calls you to account for the hope that is in you" (I Peter 3: 15 RSV). And Paul states, "Like an athlete I punish my body, treating it roughly, training it to do what it should, not what it wants to. Otherwise I fear that after enlisting others for the race, I myself might be declared unfit and ordered to stand aside" (I Corinthians 9: 27 LB).

Paul experienced what I go through night after night. Whether I'm standing on a stage talking to a crowd about Jesus, or sharing my faith one-to-one, I know that before I can even begin to speak, I've got to "clear up my bills" with the Lord. As God's witness, there is no room for unconfessed sin in my life. Like the old mountaineer who said "I 'fess 'em as I does 'em," I let God clean my slate as I go on growing in Him.

I talk to God about myself;
I talk to God about others;

and *then* I talk to others about God.
Prayer works wonders.

BE POSITIVE

Some people are always looking on the bleak side of things: a missed field goal in the fourth quarter; four putts on the eighteenth green; a seven-ten split in the tenth frame; a double-dribble call in the last half; an icing call in the third period; or a called third strike in the ninth inning. The apostle Paul disagrees:

"Set your minds on
    things that are above" (Colossians 3: 2 RSV).
"Fix your thoughts on what is
    true and good and right.
      Think about things that are
        pure and lovely,
          and dwell on the
            fine, good things in others.
Think about all you can praise God for
    and be glad about" (Philippians 4: 8 LB).

Sure, you could go up to a guy on the street and say, "Hey, buddy! You're a no good sinner and you're going to burn in hell if you don't pray with me right now to accept Jesus." Or you could be positive and talk intelligently with him, not at him, inviting him to experience the abundant life that Jesus brings to all men. Share with him the plan of salvation. Help him to understand that the Bible says to choose against Christ is to choose eternal death. Explain that God came to save the lost and not to destroy them (Luke 19: 10).

Which way do you think God can use you best: backing up to a nonbeliever and saying, "You don't want to be a Christian, do you?" or approaching him with confidence and enthusiasm, exclaiming, "Let me tell you about the greatest thing that ever happened to me"?

Be positive.

> You can't stop a smiling Christian.

Be positive.

> The very word "enthusiasm" comes from the Greek words *en* and *theos* meaning "in God."

Be positive.

> The old saying, "You can lead a horse to water but you can't make him drink," doesn't apply to Christian witnessing. If he doesn't drink at first, give him a salt tablet (Jesus said, "You are the salt of the earth") and he'll get thirsty.

Be positive.

> You are telling people not only what they need to hear, but what millions of people want to hear. One of the greatest cries going out today is, "We want peace, baby, peace." Well, tell them what the Prince of Peace said: "Peace I leave with you; my peace I give to you; not as the world gives do I give to you."

Jesus doesn't give peace in the shallow, temporary way the world knows it. It's not the kind of peace that is forcefully bought by the mutual respect various countries have for each other's missile sites. It's not the kind of peace that engraves lottery numbers on tombstones. The peace that Jesus brings doesn't deal with the symptoms (war, crime, racism, drugs, etc.); it deals with the cause —sin. James says, "What causes wars, and what causes fightings among you? Is it not your passions that are at war in your members? (James 4: 1 RSV).

Jesus brings peace where it counts: on the inside.

So be positive when you witness. You've got good news, not bad news.

BE A LISTENER

God said to Ezekiel, "I will speak with you" (Ezekiel 2: 1 RSV). But even a speaking God is frustrated and hindered unless He can find a listening man. It's because of this that God must sometimes say, "I have called and you refused to listen" (Proverbs 1: 24 RSV).

In Matthew 10: 19 God tells us "Do not be anxious how you are to speak or what you are to say; for what you are to say will be given to you . . ." (RSV). Now how can you hear what you are supposed to say when you're not listening to the one who supplies the information? As an ambassador for Christ you must:

1. Listen to God and,
2. Listen to the person you're sharing Jesus with.

I don't think I can stress enough how important it is to listen to the potential believer. Certainly his destination must be the Cross, but you've got to listen attentively to understand where he's coming from. Then you can apply Christ's answer to his specific problem.

BE HUMBLE

Nobody listens to a know-it-all. You may be privileged to be a Christian, but that doesn't mean you're a privileged character. As D. T. Niles of Ceylon said, "Evangelism is just one beggar telling another beggar where to find food." Jesus set the pace one day on the road to Jerusalem when His disciples started acting a bit holier-than-thou. He turned to them and said,

"Whoever would be great among you

must be your servant,
and whoever would be first among you
must be slave of all.
For the Son of man also came
not to be served but to serve . . ." (Mark 10:
43-45 RSV).

Don't expect the non-Christian to stick around while you beat him over the head with your Bible. If you want an audience, then take Paul's advice to Timothy:

"Again I say, don't get involved in foolish arguments which only upset people and make them angry. God's people must not be quarrelsome; they must be gentle, patient teachers of those who are wrong.

Be humble when you are trying to teach those who are mixed up concerning the truth. For if you talk meekly and courteously to them they are more likely, with God's help, to turn away from their wrong ideas and believe what is true" (II Timothy 2: 23-25 LB).

One night as I was leaving the area where we had a meeting, I heard an outbreak of yelling and loud discussion. I went over to see what was happening, and there they stood: a group of Christians surrounding a nonbeliever and his friends, heatedly arguing for their side. It was as if they were saying, "Jesus loves you. You want to fight about it?"

Be humble, Christian. There's enough hate going around without trying to drag Jesus into our fights. Besides, He doesn't have to fight. He's already won.

The Bible says "if a person isn't loving and kind, it shows that he doesn't know God—for God is love" (I John 4: 8 LB). When someone asks you whether or not you're a Christian, you can answer, "Yes, because I know God's love!"

One morning last summer I was out street-sharing

when I approached a man with "Do you know Jesus?" His allergy surfaced the second I asked.

But he started walking a little slower to reply, "Well, I go to church."

"No, mister, you don't understand," I came back at him. "Do you know Jesus?"

That was his cue to exit. By then he had concluded that I was a fanatic. He said, "Look, buddy, I've got my own religion," and walked away rapidly.

So when you are asked, "Do you know Jesus?"

Don't answer,

"I'm a deacon."

"I teach Sunday school."

"I memorized some Bible verses."

"I was baptized and confirmed."

God doesn't care if you've got the Ten Commandments tattooed on your navel.

He cares that you know the love of His Son.

And if you know it, show it!

Your attitude should be: "I'm just a nobody, telling everybody, about Somebody, who can save anybody."

BE YOURSELF

Don't try to talk to a nonbeliever the way you think Billy Graham or anyone else would. He'd be one of the first to tell you that the only person you should imitate in witnessing is the Holy Spirit. The person you are introducing to Jesus should be very important to you. See how Paul felt about his listeners:

"For what is it we live for, that gives us hope and joy and is our proud reward and crown? It is you . . . For you are our trophy and joy" (I Thessalonians 2: 19, 20 LB).

Don't let your "trophy" see you being anything but yourself. Those trophies can spot a fake everytime, and when they do, watch them run. Without knowing it, they're following the strong advice of the Bible, which tells us to beware of people who go to church but don't believe anything they hear. It says "Avoid such people" (II Timothy 3: 5 RSV).

Be yourself, Christian. Just hang loose and don't be afraid of your emotions. As Christians we must insist on being rational beings with tremendous capacities for emotional experience. We must be total men and women. The reason that most of us are afraid of emotion is that it betrays exactly where we're at and who we are. We can float in lofty abstracts and say tremendous things that sound beautiful but tell nothing of where we're really at. As "the light of the world," you *know* where you are. So be yourself when you're letting someone else know.

BE AN OBSERVER

A Christian should never say "I witness *for* Jesus." Christians are always doing things *for* Jesus; we sing for Jesus, preach for Jesus, and write for Jesus. But the Bible says, "Christ, God's faithful Son, is in complete charge of God's house. And we Christians are God's house—he lives in us" (Hebrews 3: 6 LB). If it's His house, then let Him run it and clean it. God tells us that not only do we have no power to save ourselves (Ephesians 2: 8, 9), but we also have no power to witness *for* Him: "For it is not you who speak, but the Spirit of your Father speaking through you" (Matthew 10: 20 RSV).

Be an observer.

Watch God work in you.

Be an observer.

"Keep your eyes on Jesus,
  our leader and instructor" (Hebrews 12: 2 LB).
Successful witnessing is
  Witnessing in the power of the Holy Spirit
  And leaving the results up to God.
So you don't have to worry when a chance to witness
comes along because God is ready for it.

SLIPPERY WHEN WET

"Heaven can be entered only through the narrow gate! The highway to hell is broad, and its gate is wide enough for all the multitudes who choose its easy way. But the Gateway to Life is small, and the road is narrow, and only a few ever find it" (Matthew 7: 13, 14 LB).

THE WAY OF THE CROSS is a happy one. Proverbs 16: 20 says, "Happy the man who puts his trust in the Lord" (LB). Christians don't have troubles like most people. God's Son is not a troublemaker. Instead they have problems like all people. But God's Son is a problem-solver. Therefore, anyone who bears the label "Christian" cannot afford to be ignorant of the conflicts that are erupting all over this globe.

The sign reads SLIPPERY WHEN WET and when the world is on the skids as it is today, Christians are called to apply clear thinking and compassion to help dry up the problem.

It might be all right for an ostrich to bury its head in the sand and pretend not to know what's going on around it, but a follower of Jesus has no excuse for ignorance. This chapter exposes many of the problems that cause skidding and offers an exciting alternative.

You Can Trust a "Rug Rat"

Joycie and I had just gotten in the door when the baby-sitter ran to us and said, "Oh, I'm sorry!"

I thought the worst: "Oh, no, Christopher's been killed!" With my heart in my throat I ran into the living room. There sat our eight-month-old son with an enormous blue bump on his forehead, a huge tear running down his cheek, and a great big smile on his face. He had knocked his head against the stereo, but just didn't know enough to keep crying about it. He was so beautiful; he hadn't learned yet how to milk all the sympathy he could out of a fall.

It's too bad that people learn to be deceitful. Little kids (often called rug rats) are so truthful that sometimes they are painfully blunt. One morning I was leaning against the refrigerator and drinking a glass of milk. I was physically down and felt like a truck had just flattened me. I was thinking how I needed something to pick me up and was hoping that milk would do it, when a sandy-haired little neighbor boy appeared out of nowhere and yelled, "You're ugly!" and walked away.

I said something like "Thanks, I needed that." He really made my day.

If children can be so honest, how is it that we become such good liars? I think that there are many answers.

Like It! You'll Try It!

We are bombarded and exploited by newspapers, books, television, radio, movies, magazines and everything else enterprising money mongers use to get us to buy products.

The bar of soap that almost breathes
makes us feel so alive!

The toothpaste that brightens your whole life
as well as your teeth!

The deodorant that not only keeps you dry for
years but doubles as a hair spray
and an oven cleaner.

Madison Avenue will try to get us to believe anything and most of the time it succeeds. For example, I was driving into town one day, listening to the radio, when a husky voice boomed out, "Do you have unsightly blemishes?" He went on to explain that if you had unsightly blemishes you probably wouldn't have any friends and your dating life would be zero. Like any guy sensitive about his personal appearance, I was drinking in his every word. I looked in the rear-view mirror and sure enough, there was a brand-new pimple on my left cheek. That guy had my number and I was sure that I wouldn't have a friend left if that "unsightly blemish" didn't go away.

I was so self-conscious about it that as I shopped around town that day, I was certain that all the people walking up and down the other side of the street were saying to each other, "Did you see that kid across the street with the pimple on his face?"

The influence that commercials and the media in general have in making our life styles dishonest is almost incredible.

The advertisement says, "You've come a long way, baby." That's right, baby. Now you can smoke like a man.

My goodness, if you come any further you can have our athlete's feet and bald heads. Come on girls, don't let clever jingles victimize you.

A Little Help From our Friends

I always felt that I had to look good in front of my friends. Just the thought of failing in front of them unnerved me. Do you remember how it was when your teacher returned the test papers with grades scrawled in red ink at the top of the page? The guy across from you says, "Hey, what'd you get?" covering his own paper.

"I don't know. What'd you get?" You answer, not daring to look at your grade.

"That's not fair!" he says. "I asked you first."

Although it seems comical, impressing your friends can be very dangerous. It is a tremendous motivation for you to start cheating on tests as well as on everything else.

If a girl that I was going with ever hinted that she might be thinking of dating someone else, I hurried to drop her so that I could tell the guys, *"I* broke up with *her."* Whatever the cost, I had to be cool.

A Family Affair

The sway toward dishonesty through the family is much more subtle than with the media and friends. Parents usually have good intentions but very often lovingly misguide their children.

Especially important here is the spiritual integrity of children. Certainly every parent wants to make Christmas a special experience for his little ones, but contrary to popular opinion, December 25 is not the day we celebrate the birth of a funny, little fat elf from the North Pole. It's the day Earth became the "visited planet"; when God broke through at Bethlehem. I'm not a little kid anymore, but I'm so conditioned to a tinsel Christmas that I still can't wait until the morning of the 25th to tear open my presents.

And what happens when spring rolls around? "Here comes Peter Cottontail, hoppin' down the bunny trail." It still amazes me that we can talk our children into believing that a rabbit can lay eggs.

"Look, Bobby!
  Behind the curtain over there.
    It's your Easter basket."
"Look, Linda!
  Under the television.
    It's a chocolate chicken."
"Look, family!
  On the coffee table gathering dust.
    It's the Bible,
      and it tells about a Man
        who defeated sin and death
          on this day."

TIME FOR A CHANGE

We are growing up in the midst of a technological, biological, sociological, and communications revolution. In his book, *Future Shock,* Alvin Toffler states that "In the three short decades between now and the 21st century, millions of ordinary, psychologically normal people will face an abrupt collision with the future."

I believe that the causes of the revolution that is upon us are irrevocably set in motion. The only thing that will ever stop them is the return of Christ. Ninety percent of all the scientists and engineers who have ever lived are alive today, and most of them are working on new ways to do things. They are discovering new knowledge at an incredible rate, with the total mass of knowledge almost doubling every five years! (And students wonder why school is getting tougher.)

Not long ago in Vitoria, Brazil, Jomar Henreque Silva died at the physical age of ninety although he was born only twelve years earlier. He was afflicted with progeria or precocious old age. At six months Jomar's teeth were crooked and yellow; at two his hair turned white and started falling out; at ten his skin was wrinkled and his blood vessels began to harden. He was old before his time. Likewise, with the rate of change accelerating in this decade, our children are being forced to grow up too fast and adapt to a world radically in flux.

ROCK AND ROLE

When a man came back from World War II, he was usually dedicated to making this a better world. He would exclaim, "My kids are going to have it easier than I did," and he would buckle down to work hard and pay for his family's secure little bungalow on Primrose Lane.

Bill Glasser said one day in a lecture at Wheaton College, "Dad belongs to a generation of men and women who are *goal*-oriented, but his son is part of a new generation whose members are *role*-oriented."

Think about the 50's: greasy, ducktail haircuts, black leather jackets, and combat boots. Rock 'n roll was the new thing and was it considered wild. Parents back in the '50s thought Satan had taken over for sure when the bee-bop tunes hit all the juke boxes. But compared with later acid-rock music, all that "Tutti-frutti aw rutti" and "shaboom shaboom" seems about as harmless as a Bugs Bunny cartoon.

The '60's were just about as plastic and square. I know, because those were my teenage years. You were cool if you had a lot of class and money. It was important to impress one another. Cheerleaders and football heroes had automatic status and were really in. You also had it made if you had flashy clothes and a car. This whole scene was just about as ridiculous as one of those beach party movies starring Frankie Avalon and Annette Funicello.

It's not hard to see why this Joe-College routine finally changed. If you had "unsightly blemishes," tacky clothes, and no money to dish out for a heavy date, all the strikes were against you.

Eventually kids began to rebel. Today's generation of guys and girls have almost totally made the switch from goal-orientation to role-orientation. You are asking "Who am I?" and "Why am I alive?" You are questioning some of the sacred cows that your parents have let out to pasture.

Youth cry to their elders:

"Your make-believe world is like a big white cloud.

It looks good from a distance,
but when you get up to it,
there's not much there.

You run around acting busy and important,
when at any second
some maniac could push a button
and blow the entire thing to bits."

Youth say:

"You think nothing of getting a divorce
and fouling up the lives of the children
you leave behind.

You pretend to love each other in public,
but drive us crazy with your
fighting at home."

Youth claim:

"You tell us not to march and get violent,
and throw rocks through administration

windows,
but you order planes to bomb
the innocent villages of Quang Tri
and An Loc."

Youth cry out:
"You spend millions of dollars building
cold cathedrals
and chilly churches.
You have the audacity to hire professional
Christians
who can only read proper prayer,
and recite proper sermons.
You tell us the Ground of All Being is
the Unmoved Mover
and the Divine Other.
You pay scant homage to God,
and you wonder why we seek spiritual experiences with pot and LSD."

Youth shout:
"You gave us the pill and Playboy,
and now you decry our morals.
Every time we open our eyes
we see nothing but skin and sexy ads.
You have made your little girl the target
for every male biological urge in the country.
Why are you surprised when she comes home
pregnant?"

The way American parents manipulate their children
to make dollars is a crime. They rape their morals and
seduce their minds with television commercials and adver-
tising, as they pound it into their heads that:
"If you only have one life to live,
live it as a blond."

No! I have only one life to live, but the Bible says I

can go on living it forever if I love Jesus (I John 2: 25).
"You should escape

and come on over to a cola."

No soft drink can save you. Come on over to Jesus Christ. He's the real thing.

I'm glad it was the Lord's plan for me to be born and to live in America. There are some countries that would crucify me for my stand for Christ. But as a citizen of Heaven first and foremost, I must declare that America will never be God's country until we are God's people. I don't believe that Jesus Christ is the prime minister of the United States or any other country of the world. God is not a White, Anglo-Saxon, Protestant marching through the suburbs of Chicago, carrying an attache case filled with beer brewed in "God's country." He is a Holy God who challenges:

"If my people who are called by my name

humble themselves,

and pray and seek my face,

and turn from their wicked ways,

then I will hear from heaven,

and will forgive their sin

and heal their land" (II Chronicles 7: 14 RSV).

The Bible also says that when Jesus comes back, "So shall he startle many nations; kings shall shut their mouths because of him" (Isaiah 52: 15 RSV). So let the kings, presidents, and rulers of the nations of this world take care.

WHAT'S LIFE ALL ABOUT?

In the meantime, youth are asking the right questions: Who am I? Why am I here? What is my purpose in life? Who will tell them that Jesus said, "I am the Way, the

Truth, and the Life"?

Consider this little drama:

SON: What is life all about, dad?"

DAD: Well, son, life is going to school and getting that diploma.

SON: What for, dad?

DAD: Well, so you can make a good living when you get out in the world.

SON: But why, dad?

DAD: Well, so you can be well-off when you retire.

SON: What for, dad?

DAD: Well . . . uh . . . so that when you die, your children will be well cared for . . . and that's what life's all about.

SON: No, dad, that can't be what life's all about. Not when so many people are starving to death all over the world. Not when little babies are being chewed to pieces by rats every night in our nation's ghettoes. Not when thousands of guys and girls are pumping their bodies so full of chemicals that they not only destroy the neurons of their brains, but also their capacity to love and be loved. I love you dad, and I know you have sacrificed a lot for me. But you can keep my Mickey Mouse watch, and my alligator-covered radio from Florida, and my spiffy new wardrobe. *I want to know what life's really about.* We can put a man on the moon, but we can't live in peace together. What can we possibly do about war, hatred, hunger, poverty, racism and bigotry?

THE CHILD WHO NEVER GREW UP

Standing in the middle of this world stage is a gentle but bold carpenter from Galilee who says, "What does it profit a man, to gain the whole world and forfeit his life?" (Mark 8: 36 RSV). There's more to life than a two-car garage, a color television, wall-to-wall carpeting, and central air-conditioning. "Vanity of vanities, says the Preacher, vanity of vanities! All is vanity. . . . I have seen everything that is done under the sun; and behold, all is vanity . . ." (Ecclesiastes 1: 2, 14 RSV).

We continue being and rearing a generation of helpless children. This child that never grows up is our responsibility because we have taught him how to make a living but not how to live.

We're all to blame for this eternal infant because each of us makes him what he is. He's many different people; he's all people. He's

. . . a sixteen-year-old boy shooting heroin under his tongue with a filthy syringe;

. . . a run-away girl sexually assaulted on her first night in the big city;

. . . a sports-crazy father who spends more time watching football on television than investing love in his own family;

. . . a middle-aged mother who plays bridge with the girls while her children are total strangers to God's love;

. . . a seasoned clergyman who learned long ago that it doesn't pay to preach the Gospel.

A therapist at a maximum security prison recently told me, "the family backgrounds of these prisoners are unbelievable. Their problems almost always go back to a common-law marriage or a broken home."

It's as true today as it ever was: messed-up families produce messed-up kids. I'm not saying that our children will be any better parents than we are, because without Jesus they won't. David Wilkerson states, "I know there is a great lack in most families in this day. I know, because many of the thousands of teenagers that I contact in my ministry have gotten into problems because of a deficiency in their family life, Christian or non-Christian."

The problems revealed in this chapter remind us that the wrong road through life can be slippery, very slippery. Traveling its way breeds all kinds of trouble—fighting, division, generation gaps.

But there are answers. There is a way to bridge these gaps for good, a way to make people united rather than divided. The Bible says,

"Teach a child to choose the right path,

and when he is older he will remain upon it"

(Proverbs 22: 6 LB).

But what is the right path? Try following the one that bears this road sign: DIVIDED HIGHWAY ENDS.

DIVIDED HIGHWAY ENDS

"In all your ways acknowledge him, and he will make straight your paths" (Proverbs 3: 6 RSV).

WHAT A SIGHT! The entire Laurent family filed out of their pew and went down to the front of the church where they turned and faced the congregation.

I don't know why I had cold chills. After all, we'd agreed beforehand that when the preacher gave the invitation to become members of the church, we would all go forward and join up.

I was so self-conscious I couldn't raise my head. I stared at my shoes and decided to wait this one out. I thought it would be over after the preacher prayed, but he went on to tell the people to come down and give us a friendly welcome. Oh, no! The thought of all those strangers button-holing me was more than I could take, but I was in for a happy surprise. These people who pumped our hands in greeting didn't act like strangers. Their genuine enthusiasm and great warmth melted my icy aloofness, and I was caught up in the joyful spirit of making friends.

I noticed one sweet old lady making her way down our family's receiving line. She was talking to my brother, Bill, and without even asking his name, she said, "It's wonderful to have you here today, *Andrew.*"

Andrew? I thought, "Lady, his name's not Andrew. He's my brother, Bill."

Then she turned and headed toward me.

"Hello there, little Peter," she said.

"Lady, my name's not Peter. I'm Bob!"

I was certain that she wasn't playing with a full deck, but then her explanation was really something else. She said, "I called your brother 'Andrew' because he asked you to come to church with him today, and Andrew was the disciple who went back and asked his brother, Peter, to go with him to meet Jesus."

That was one of the most beautiful things I had ever heard. I was thrilled. "Hey, everybody. That's my brother, Andrew, over there. And I'm Peter!"

I had made up my mind that church was a terrific place to be. I looked around at everyone smiling and being nice to the rest of my family. I felt good inside. I felt like crying.

But it didn't last.

INSTANT REPLAY

A friend of mine once told me that Americans are "ten-day" people. He said that we're spacey, fly-by-night, and wish-washy; we have instant potatoes, instant coffee, instant breakfast, instant love, and instant religion. We get excited about something and our enthusiasm lasts about ten days. I think he's right. My family's "passion for piety" hardly made it past the first potluck supper.

A Sunday morning at our house would soon show that

the carriage had turned back into a pumpkin. Mom would come into our bedroom early and announce "time to get up for church, boys."

"Aw, mom. We stayed up late last night watching Creature Features. Can't we sleep in today, please?"

"I said it's time to get up for church, boys!"

"Aw, mom. I don't feel very good. My stomach hurts. And I think I've got a fever. Yeh, I do. Feel my forehead; it's hot."

"Well, your little rearend's going to be a whole lot hotter if you don't get out of that bed and get ready for church!"

I got up.

Then the real competition began. All of us kids went into the kitchen and fought over who got the Sugar Crisp in the Kellogg's Variety Pack. Then we fought over who got the Sunday funnies. Then we trooped to the bathroom and fought over the mirror. We fought all the way to church, walked down the aisle, hot and sweaty, and took over the Laurent pew for another time of "worship."

I challenge any minister in the country to match the action we already had before we got to the doors of the church. And our poor preacher! You know, clergymen come under a lot of criticism—some deserved, some not—and I'm certainly not averse to pointing out their frailties myself. They're frequent targets for all of us to take potshots at, partly because they make such easy targets. Unlike the rest of us, a minister has a couple of hundred people going over his person with a fine-toothed comb, looking for flaws (I don't know about you, but nobody needs a comb to find mine). The position of pastor is a high privilege and should be valued by the man who is called to it. Let's have a little more empathy for the "exhausted ecclesiastics," the "played-out preachers," and the "ready-to-drop reverends" who are tired of beating their heads against the brick walls of their congregations' faithlessness; who grow weary of figuring out ways to get the saints off their seats.

INSUFFICIENT INFORMATION

Our pastor had his work cut out for him that morning. Somehow he was supposed to make spiritual giants out of the six of us, when we were doing good to be religious dwarfs.

You could set your watch by when I fell asleep in church. For awhile I'd watch my sister drawing on the back of one of the church registration cards. Then I'd try to get somebody up in the choir loft to smile at me. After that I'd read the bulletin for the fourth time and count all the misspelled words. But, inevitably, drowsiness would win. I didn't want the preacher to notice that I was sleeping, so I would sit forward, bow my head on the pew in front of me, and hope that he thought I was praying.

As if he didn't know what was going on.

What had happened to us? We were so full of life at the beginning. How did we get into the rut of playing church?

We suffered from insufficient information. Someone told us about John 3: 16, that if we believed in Jesus we would never perish, but have everlasting life. None of us wanted to die; we all wanted to go to Heaven. We believed in God, of course. So we joined the local community of believers. How come it wasn't working out? Hadn't we done everything right?

The answer to that is an unequivocal NO. We were wrong because we hadn't let God do anything. Someone should have informed us of the context from which John 3: 16 is taken.

In the third chapter of John, Jesus tells Nicodemus, a very religious man, that he would never get into the Kingdom of God unless he was first born again. Nicodemus replied, "Do you mean that I have to go back into my mother's womb and start all over again?"

Jesus told him, "Truly, truly I say to you, unless one is born of water and the Spirit, he cannot enter the kingdom of God."

In other words, you must first be born of water—a physical birth—the normal process observed during every human birth. Then you must let God give life to you as He enters your being by way of the Holy Spirit. This spiritual birth—being born again—is a whole new ball game.

I BELIEVE "INTO" JESUS

We had spent all of our family life together believing in God without being born again because we didn't understand what it means to believe. I was sitting in Greek class at seminary one day when I came upon *pisteuo* meaning "to believe." The lesson said that whenever the Greeks used the verb "to believe" with reference to God, they would follow it with the infinitive *eis* meaning "into." When a believer in New Testament times wanted to attest to his faith, he would say *Pisteuo eis ton Kurion,* which translated means, "I believe into the Lord." This thought hit me like a ton of bricks; I got so excited I almost fell off my chair. It's one thing to say nonchalantly, "I believe in Jesus," and quite another to claim, "I believe into Jesus."

I can believe in an airplane, that it is there and that it

can lift my weight. But until I believe "into" it and actually get on board, my belief will get me nowhere.

I can believe in Santa Claus, George Washington, or Alfred E. Newman, but that belief gives me no power to change my life eternally. However, I can believe "into" Jesus Christ and experience His authority to forgive my sins and make me a new creation. In New Testament language, "believe" is an action word and it points to a Gospel of action:

"So faith by itself, if it has no works, is dead" (James 2: 17 RSV).

"You will know them by their fruits" (Matthew 7: 16 RSV).

"But be doers of the word, and not hearers only" (James 1: 22 RSV).

My family was missing out on abundant living because we just did not know *enough* about God's requirements and fantastic promises. I really don't think this was the fault of any pastor, or the music ministry, or a Sunday school department. The real culprit was our own ignorance and according to law, that is no excuse.

Eventually we all must answer for our own sin. When Jesus comes in judgment, nobody's going to volunteer to take our place in hell. But God has already taken the place on the Cross that you and I deserve. If we refuse to accept this substitutionary death, then we are going to have to go it our own way.

LOVE BEATS LOLLIPOPS

Not long ago I read an article in a Chicago newspaper about the problems that stepmothers have with their children. It said,

In many families where a stepchild is present, religion

is a major problem. But to a New York woman recently interviewed, whose five "his, hers, and our" children were at one time being raised in three religious faiths, religion is the least of her problems. "It's the day-to-day living that gets me down," said the mother.

This woman represents millions of other people, and accurately reflects what my family was like. We were rubbing shoulders with God who could add tremendously to our day-to-day living and we didn't even recognize His love. What a difference that could have made. Instead we went on struggling to keep the loose ends of our family together. And without His guidance, chaos is inevitable.

In *Get Your Hands Off My Throat,* David Wilkerson writes,

Today's kids have been so baptized in "things" they have developed marshmallow philosophies. Seldom needing to make choices or decisions, they learn to postpone things. They have learned how to enjoy the pleasures heaped upon them by doting parents but have not been taught to cope with pain. There is no challenge to develop a will, so they are often easily led by rebels and drug abusers. "Instamatic" family atmosphere has tired both generations and left everyone bewildered that so much wealth could cause so much misery.

Wilkerson reveals a valuable fact here: we can sacrifice and work for years in order to give our children the things that we never had, but unless those gifts include Jesus, we are really giving them nothing.

Ephesians 6: 1 says, "Children, obey your parents." So when Junior behaves himself we give him a lollipop. When he's a little older and behaves himself, gets good grades, and stays away from drugs, we reward him again with a new car for his birthday.

What's wrong with us? When are we going to learn that we can't buy off our children? They don't need money as much as they need good, old-fashioned *love*. And the only kind of love that lasts beyond the hour and beyond the grave is the love of Jesus Christ.

Ephesians 6: 4 goes on to say, "And now a word to you parents. Don't keep on scolding and nagging your children, making them angry and resentful. Rather, bring them up with the loving discipline the Lord himself approves, with suggestions and godly advice" (LB).

It doesn't matter how good our intentions are in bringing up our kids outside of God's love. Good intentions will never replace good instruction. Children will go their way and parents theirs, while the only road which leads to healing and union is God's way, marked by the sign, DIVIDED HIGHWAY ENDS. The results of a family life without Jesus will soon show up.

The Bible reminds us, "Do not be deceived; God is not mocked, for whatever a man sows, that he will also reap" (Galatians 6: 7 RSV).

It's no wonder that so many families split apart at the seams. Mine was no exception. I think I had pretty terrific parents, but my mom and dad couldn't begin to build out of our shortcomings something that only God can create: a together family.

Eugene Austill, a forty-five-year-old father from Buckeye, Arizona, wanted to bring his family back together, and he made the headlines trying. He had a friend crucify him on a twelve-foot cross, hoping that his family would rally around him out of sympathy. The friend said that Austill screamed in terror as the nails were driven into his feet and hands. He hanged there for two hours before police finally found him. But his family reunion never did come off. Only God can complete a family, and man's attempt to do God's work often looks pretty ridiculous.

PETE AND REPETE

I'll bet Austill's family started out like most families. In the beginning the father and mother are idolized by the children. They're superheroes who can do no wrong. A little kid worships his parents and tries to be just like them.

My boy, Christopher, imitates me in every way he can. I frown and he frowns; I smile and he giggles; I'm Pete and he's Repete.

And so every young boy watches his dad with adoring eyes:

He watches him light up a cigarette,
  and can't wait to fill his lungs
    with that same gray warmth.
Maybe one day he'll even be able to surpass him,
  and blow marijuana circles in the air.
He watches him guzzle a six-pack
  during a television doubleheader,
    and is grateful for the few sips he gives
    him.
Maybe one day he'll be able to hold his booze
  as well as our eight million alcoholics do.

I can't begin to count the number of kids who have come to me in the past few years and asked me to pray with them about their mom and dad. All of a sudden these young people have got problem parents on their hands. Rearing non-Christian parents is one of the hardest things a Christian kid can try to do.

Joyce and I can hardly wait for the day when our son comes to us and says, "Well, mom and dad, you're not the

112

only Jesus-people in this family anymore."

The Bible says that it is dad's responsibility to be the spiritual leader of the family. And mom is his helpmate.

FINALLY A P. K.

In my first year at seminary, I asked God to make my family complete, and He's been working on it ever since. About four years ago, my father, who had been faithfully reading his Bible every morning and evening for a couple of years, finally caught on fire and decided to let God have His way from then on.

The things that happened in my parents' lives after dad gave God the steering wheel would fill another book. The Lord not only did the steering, but he pushed His foot down on the accelerator as well, and my folks haven't stopped racing since. They sold their house in Springfield, Illinois; dad quit his job after twenty-eight years, and they moved to Chicago. There dad enrolled in Moody Bible Institute in spite of the fact that he was six years over their age limit. He was graduated and guess what that makes me after all this time—a P. K.—a preacher's kid!

Larry Christenson says in *The Christian Family,*
Happy is the child who happens in upon his parent from time to time to see him on his knees, who sees mother and father rising early, or going aside regularly, to keep times with the Lord. That child has learned a lesson no lecture could impart. He has seen that God matters—He's important enough to take up our time.

A friend called me long distance one night to relate a wonderful experience she'd just had. She told me that she had inadvertently passed by her mother's bedroom and had seen through the half-open door that her mother was kneeling by the bed talking to God. This sight did more for that girl's relationship with her mother than a thousand discussions on the generation gap could. Besides, Jesus closes that gap and makes it nonexistent. She saw a new side of her mother, and for the first time in her life, started to understand the woman that had brought her into the world. Their divided highway had come to an end.

Let your children see Jesus working in you. Let God make your family a part of His "forever family."

"Believe in the Lord Jesus,
  and you will be saved,
    you and your household" (Acts 16: 31 RSV).

Once you have taken this step of believing *into* Jesus Christ, you have received a gift of eternal life that can never be taken away, and you are heading on a road that cannot be detoured; a road that boasts the sign NO "U" TURN.

NO U TURN

And a main road will go through that once-deserted land; it will be named "The Holy Highway." No evil-hearted men may walk upon it. God will walk there with you; even the most stupid cannot miss the way. No lion will lurk along its course, nor will there be any other dangers; only the redeemed will travel there. These, the ransomed of the Lord, will go home along that road to Zion, singing the songs of everlasting joy. For them all sorrow and all sighing will be gone forever; only joy and gladness will be there (Isaiah 35: 8-10 LB).

WE HELD the first annual Good News Circle School for Evangelism at a beautiful conference grounds in Green Lake, Wisconsin. The key verse of the week was "Teach these great truths to trustworthy men who will, in turn, pass them on to others" (II Timothy 2: 2 LB), and I was very excited about the chance to do some in-depth teaching on the great Biblical themes. I was especially proud that I had scheduled a meeting concerning "The Holy Spirit in Evangelism." (How's that for programing the Holy Spirit?) I thought that I had enough of the right material to cover all of the important areas, but God used the greatest light show I'd ever seen to teach me otherwise.

OH, HOLY NIGHT

I call this the "Night of the Second Coming Covenant." It was about 10:30 when over two hundred of us walked out of the rustic old hayloft where we held our evening programs into the cool Wisconsin night. Suddenly one of the kids shouted, "Look!" Responding as one, our group was electrified by the sight of the Northern Lights, the Aurora Borealis, arching its vivid blues, greens, and reds across the sky. We stood there breathless as it continued to change form, pulsating its way from the North to the West. We were totally captivated by its awesomeness as we watched its rays slowly etch their way up . . . up . . . up . . . like fingers pointing to the apex of the sky.

Just then a girl cried out, "Jesus is coming!"

I stood there stunned.

We stayed outside for hours that night, praying, talking about the Second Coming, and thanking God for His sign. No one is ever going to convince us that God didn't hang up those lights especially for us as a covenant of His Second Coming. My only concern was what we could do as an encore next year, because there's only one way He could top that!

CATCHING UP

Later I went to my room and sat in the dark for a long time, thinking. Why had I never seriously considered the

117

return of Christ before? How come I didn't really know anything about it? I remembered having sat across from John Wesley White at a restaurant the very night God gave him the title of his fantastic book about the second advent of Jesus: *Re-Entry.* I was naturally pleased for him, but was hardly turned-on by his subject. I figured that anybody with two earned doctorates couldn't be expected to write about anything very relevant anyway.

Not relevant! How wrong could I have been? God was just beginning to show me that Jesus' coming again is as relevant as tomorrow's newspaper. I had some catching up to do.

I began immediately to research the Second Coming, starting with Andre Cole's uncoverings and working my way up to a heavier study of William Biederwolf's *The Second Coming Bible.* I could hardly believe that the Second Coming is mentioned 380 times in the New Testament, and dealt with in some way over 1850 times in the entire Bible. Seven out of every ten chapters and 23 out of 27 books in the New Testament refer to it. How can we Bible believers know so little about what we believe?

THE HOLY HIGHWAY

Time and again the New Testament calls the Second Coming the "blessed hope" (Titus 2: 13). Early Christians didn't greet one another by saying, "Hey, did you see the new tunic Demetrius bought for his wife?" or "Was I ever lucky to get seats for the gladiator fights right on the fifty yard line."

Instead they warmly welcomed each other with a friendly "Maranatha," which means, "The Lord is coming." This was their confidence, that in the middle of a world gripped with evil, in the middle of terrible suffering and persecution, there is a road upon which Christians will go home, singing songs of everlasting joy. Its travelers will know no sorrow and only gladness will be there. It is the holy highway (Isaiah 35: 8) and is well marked by the road sign, NO "U" TURN. The first century believers held on to Christ's coming as their hope, the blessed hope.

Should his reappearance be any less important to us today? As the nihilistic giants we face every day—racism, poverty, crime, bigotry, drug abuse—threaten to stomp us into the ground, we can stand firm in the promise that Jesus is coming to usher in a bright new world, where there will be no more death, mourning, crying, or pain (Revelation 21: 4).

And the fantastic fact is that it could happen any time. This is why Jesus said, "Therefore you also must be ready; for the Son of man is coming at an hour you do not expect" (Matthew 24: 44 RSV). We are to be on the alert at all times. This was the message underlying His parable of the ten virgins. "Those who were ready went" (Matthew 25: 1-12).

Nearly two thousand years ago, Earth's schedule was interrupted by the living God. It was His first coming, and Jesus lived, died, and then lived again. Before He left, He said that He would come again at a time when it would appear that we were wiping one another off the face of the earth. In his own words, "unless those days are shortened, all mankind will perish. But they will be shortened for the sake of God's chosen people" (Matthew 24: 22 LB).

His disciples said, "Tell us, when will this be, and what will be the sign of your coming and of the close of the age?" (Matthew 24: 3 RSV.) He told them that no one knows the date or the hour when the end will be, except the Father (Matthew 24: 36). But He proceeded to give them many signs, and stated that when we see these signs, we will know that His return is near, even at the doors (Matthew 24: 34).

As we review some of these signs, it seems certain to me that we are racing toward the last events of history.

ISRAEL IN THE NEWS

For over three thousand years, the Bible has affirmed that Christ's coming and history's last episode would be written around the nation of Israel. In the nineteenth century and half way through the twentieth, those who spoke of the immediacy of the Second Coming were laughed at and mocked, and understandably so. After all, Israel wasn't even a nation—yet.

On May 14, 1948, to the amazement of the watching world, Israel received her nationhood. But Jerusalem was still held captive, as Jesus said it would be until the end (Luke 21: 24). You can imagine the excitement when, in the Six-Day War in June, 1967, the bold Israel army, outnumbered eighty-to-one, captured old Jerusalem, ending a bondage of 2,553 years.

Nearly 5,000 years ago, God told us through the prophet Zechariah that Israel would become the center of trouble for the world after it once again became a nation (Zechariah 12: 1-3). Isaiah 2: 2 (LB) says, "In the last days Jerusalem and the Temple of the Lord will become the world's greatest attraction." One of President Nixon's advisers once told him, "The Middle East situation is the most serious and complex problems of our century, which could launch a third world war."

In 1446 BC God told Moses what would happen to the Jewish people from his day to the present time. These prophecies have been flawlessly fulfilled to the letter. The Middle East is now set up for the last climactic event. *Maranatha!*

SECOND-COMING POLITICS

At the time of the end, the Bible says that a ten-nation confederacy will be formed out of the old Roman Empire (Daniel 7: 23-28). This alliance will begin its take-over of the world under the genius of an electrifying man. The Bible calls him the Anti-Christ, and says that the world will call him its Messiah.

This confederacy certainly appears to be the present European Common Market. Hal Lindsay, author of *The Late Great Planet Earth,* not long ago came back from a session of the Market and announced that their plans coincide perfectly with Bible prophecy. He said he felt like a divine spy at the meeting and as he listened to their projections, he could hardly believe that he was actually watching prophecy being fulfilled. There are now nine nations officially in the confederacy. The Bible says that the capital of the confederacy is to be Rome (Revelation 17: 18). Andre Cole reports that some time ago Rome was selected to be the future headquarters of the European Common Market.

Do Chapters 38 and 39 of Ezekiel predict Russia's present hatred for the new state of Israel and her later invasion of this little country? There is some pretty convincing evidence that the Scriptures are speaking of Russia, both from linguistic considerations and from the geographical location of that country as the great power directly north of Palestine. Lindsay and Cole remind us that Meshech is the ancient name of Moscow, and Tubal is present day Tobolsk, the former capital of Russia.

Wilhelm Genenius, a great Hebrew scholar of the early nineteenth century, says that this prophecy undoubtedly speaks of the Russian people.

According to Scofield,

That the primary reference is to the northern European powers, headed up by Russia, all agree . . . The reference to Meshech and Tubal (Moscow and Tobolsk) is a clear mark of identification. Russia and the northern powers have been the latest persecutors of dispersed Israel, and it is congruous both with divine justice and with the covenants that justice should fall at the climax of the last mad attempt to exterminate the remnant of Israel in Jerusalem.

The book of Revelation describes a vast Eastern army (Revelation 16: 12-16; 9: 16) that marches westward over the Euphrates River and adds its 200 million men to the holocaust of the last war of the world, the Battle of Armageddon.

Such an enormous army was unthinkable in the past. Who possibly could field a military force as large as the population of the United States? But recently on a television documentary called "The Voice of the Dragon," Red China boasted of having an army of over 200 million men. An Associated Press release came up with the same figures.

Jesus said that before the end, wars would increase in frequency and intensity, just as birth pangs heighten before birth (Matthew 24: 6-8). Now get these statistics:

1. In World War I, eight million, five hundred thousand men were killed.
2. In World War II, over 52 million were killed.
3. Since World War II, there have been 44 wars, twelve of them considered major.
4. The Joint Chiefs of Staff say that there are at least

twenty-five trouble spots around the globe where another Vietnam could break out overnight.

In his famous song about the Second Coming, Larry Norman says,

"Life was filled with guns and wars
    and everyone got trampled on the floor . . .
        I wish we'd all been ready."

More Signs of Life

Jesus said, ". . . there will be famines and earthquakes in many places" (Matthew 24: 7 LB). In the past two years there has been an earthquake somewhere in the world on every day but two! A renowned seismologist tells us that there has been a 2000 percent increase in the frequency of earthquakes over the past 400 years.

Over ten thousand people starve to death daily. In a period of five days, more people die of starvation than the entire American death toll from the Vietnam War. Stanford biologist Paul Ehrlich and Ohio State University's Bruce Griffing feel that we may have no more than a decade before famine is universal.

"But the day of the Lord will come like a thief . . . and the elements will be dissolved with fire, and the earth and the works that are upon it will be burned up" (II Peter 3: 10 RSV). This verse was scoffed at until the advent of the atomic bomb, but now it and many others written at a time when man's deadliest weapon was a sword, seem to be describing the results of a thermonuclear war (Zechariah 14: 12).

". . . the end times, when travel and education shall be vastly increased!" (Daniel 12: 4 LB). I have already mentioned in this book the phenomenal knowledge explosion, in which total knowledge is almost doubling every five years. As far as travel goes, this space age of ours is certainly in line with the last age.

". . . wickedness is multiplied . . ." (Matthew 24: 12). Crime is presently increasing far faster than the growth in population.

"For the time is coming when people will not endure sound teaching, but having itching ears they will accumulate for themselves teachers to suit their own likings, and will turn away from listening to the truth and wander into myths" (II Timothy 4: 3, 4 RSV). Consider the booming interest in astrology, reincarnation, seances, palm reading, and many other flights into the supernatural.

"And this gospel of the kingdom will be preached throughout the whole world, as a testimony to all nations; and then the end will come" (Matthew 24: 14 RSV). Perhaps this is the most exciting sign of all. After seeing representatives of over two hundred nations claiming their individual countries for Christ at Explo '72, I knew for certain that the fulfillment of this prophecy was at hand. With radio, television, the printed page, and other sophisticated means of communication, this shrinking planet of ours is hearing about the Good News of the Kingdom.

Maranatha!

The Lord is coming!

About those who saw all these signs, Jesus said, "Truly, I say to you, this generation will not pass away till all these things take place" (Matthew 24: 34 RSV). Jesus is coming again, and He promises, "I go to prepare a place for you. And if I go and prepare a place for you, I will come again, and receive you unto myself" (John 14: 2, 3 KJV).

Paul says, "the Lord himself will come down from heaven with a mighty shout and with the soul-stirring cry of the archangel and the great trumpet-call of God" (I Thessalonians 4: 16 LB).

John says, "he is coming with the clouds, and every eye will see him" (Revelation 1: 7 RSV).

Jesus says, "I am Alpha and Omega, the beginning and the ending, saith the Lord, which is, and which was, and which is to come" (Revelation 1: 8 KJV).

Maranatha! This is our Blessed Hope!

A DAY TO REMEMBER

But you say, "This whole thing really frustrates me! I want to get married first . . . or get that raise in salary . . . or take a vacation . . . or raise my family . . . then Jesus can come again."

The very last aspiration of the Scripture demonstrates how all of us believers should feel about His coming. Jesus said, "Surely I am coming soon," and John replied, "Amen. Come, Lord Jesus!"

Those early believers weren't waiting around for the undertaker, they were living for the uppertaker. When they parted from each other, they didn't have to say goodbye. They could say, "See you later—here, there, or in the air."

This is the ultimate event to look forward to. Just think, if you girls can get so excited about a new wardrobe, I can't imagine your reaction to getting a new body! (I Corinthians 14: 52, 53.)

Rather than fearing this "terrible Day of the Lord" in the Jewish tradition, we are to rejoice at its arrival:

"But you are not in darkness, brethren,
    for that day to surprise you like a thief.
        For you are all sons of light and sons of the
        day . . .

So then let us not sleep,
    as others do,
        but let us keep awake . . ."
            (I Thessalonians 5: 4, 5 RSV).

As children of the light and of the day, we Christians have nothing to fear. We must be on the watch for His return.

HERE COME DE JUDGE

But what about you? Jesus said that He is coming again, but this time as a judge. Will you lightly pass over the overwhelming evidence for the return of Jesus, and shrug it off as some fanatical Christian scheme, or will you receive it for what it is: a fact, every bit as real as His first coming? The choice is now yours.

You can run from God until you think you have
left Him far behind.
    But He will always outdistance you and
    patiently wait for you to run His way.
You can be apathetic to His message and try to stay
totally neutral.
    But when the important questions catch up to
    you He remains the only answer.
You can continue to say NO to His love, but He
will keep on loving you and if He is forced to
leave you alone, that's exactly what you'll be,
alone.
    You can persist in clutching a passport
    marked "Destination: Hell."
        Or you can put in your reservation right
        now for the Eternal Trip by calling on the
        Name of the Lord and following Jesus.
        "Awake, O sleeper, and arise from the

126

dead, and Christ shall give you light"
(Ephesians 5: 14 RSV).

Larry Norman, one of the major spokesmen for the Jesus movement in America, ends his song with:

"There's no time to change your mind.

How could you have been so blind?

The Father spoke,

The demons dined,

The Son has come,

And you've been left behind.

I wish we'd all been ready."

An old Chinese proverb says, "The journey of a thousand miles begins with one step." Now step onto that "holy highway" and if you heed its road signs of life, you'll also be saying "WHAT A WAY TO GO."

From David C. Cook Publishing Co.

"We don't want to FAIL!"

Surely that expresses the sentiment of parents today—and here's competent help. Jay Kesler's book offers a new path of family harmony through the trying (and universal) growing-up experiences . . .

* Coming of age
* Discipline and love
* "Everybody's doing it!"
* Drugs, alcohol, tobacco
* Church relationship

This advice exposes the roots of parent-child differences!

72660—$1.25

You can order this book from your bookstore, or from the David C. Cook Publishing Co., Elgin, IL 60120 (in Canada: Weston, Ont. M9L 1T4).

--- USE THIS COUPON ---------------------------

Name _____

Address _____

City _____ State _____ ZIP Code _____

TITLE	STOCK NO.	PRICE	QTY.	SUB-TOTAL
Let's Succeed with Our Teenagers	72660	$1.25		$

NOTE: On orders placed with David C. . . . . Handling
Cook Publishing Co., add handling
charge of 25¢ for first dollar, plus   **TOTAL** $
5¢ for each additional dollar.